D1458512

Unionism Decayed
1997 – 2007

by

David Vance

authorHOUSE®

AuthorHouse™ UK Ltd.
500 Avebury Boulevard
Central Milton Keynes, MK9 2BE
www.authorhouse.co.uk
Phone: 08001974150

First published by AuthorHouse 3/29/2008

ISBN: 978-1-4343-6471-5 (sc)

Library of Congress Control Number: 2008900538

Printed in the United States of America
Bloomington, Indiana

This book is printed on acid-free paper.

ACKNOWLEDGEMENT

I want to start by saying that this book would not have been possible without the immense support of my wife, Hilary. She has encouraged me all along the way, helped whenever I have faltered and has offered insights that have been of profound value to my pulling together the disparate threads that constitute this book. Above all else she has been there for me from start to finish. I dedicate this book to her with all my love.

I would also like to acknowledge the generous help of my American friend Alan Frost, grandson of Harry Frost (who signed the Ulster Covenant) and nephew of Archie McDonald (who was killed in the Belfast Blitz).

Finally, I would also like to thank all those readers from my website www.atangledweb.squarespace.com who have kindly offered their encouragement along the way.

INTRODUCTION

"You may gain temporary appeasement by a policy of concession to violence, but you do not gain lasting peace that way"

Anthony Eden

Surely the political consensus is clear? The peace process in Northern Ireland has been a good thing. It has helped resolve a centuries old conflict and saved many lives. It is now celebrated around the world. Those politicians who have assisted in the drive to ensure the peace has lasted are visionary and courageous. It can even act as a template that can be used in other conflict situations. Northern Ireland has emerged from the dark shadows of terrorism into the sunny blue skies of a land built on the firm principles of peace. The Union between Northern Ireland and Great Britain is secured and even Irish republicans accept this. Unionists have never enjoyed such success and now wield real influence.

Forget it.

The so-called "peace process" is nothing of the sort. For well over ten years, Northern Ireland has been turned into a debauched political laboratory in which the tenets of democracy have been eviscerated, terrorists have been rewarded, murderers have been hailed as heroes, the rule of law has been humbled and justice has been dispensed with. It's appeasement on a Chamberlain-scale embraced by a grasping unprincipled local political elite.

This is the book that spells out why the peace is a false one. It dissents from the view that power-sharing with terrorists is a necessary evil. It makes it clear why so many unionist politicians have shown a fatal lack of resolve to stand fast on their solemn promises. Above all else it concerns itself with the way in which unionism has changed over the past ten years; it's about the decay of unionism.

During this period I have been able to observe from inside and outside how the peace processors have corrupted the spirit of political unionism. The ascendancy of IRA/Sinn Fein to its current position of sitting in the government of Northern Ireland represents the triumph of the tyrant and it's time to consider why unionism has facilitated this.

CONTENTS

IN HUMPTY DUMPTY LAND

If there is one thing in life worse than being a unionist, it is being a unionist that has consistently opposed the provisions of the Belfast Agreement/Good Friday Agreement. Well at least that is what it has felt like these past ten years and I suspect that I may not be the only unionist who feels this way.

For as long as I can remember, unionists have had a poor press, frequently portrayed as being just marginally more advanced than the cannibal practicing Korowai tribe in Papua, New Guinea, though without the appeal of persecuted minority status!

But after years of misrepresentation and vilification, from 1997 onwards a certain type of unionist began to get a much more positive media treatment. Those who embraced the provisions of the Belfast Agreement/Good Friday Agreement were portrayed as progressives, enlightened souls prepared to move on from the intransigence of the past. However those who rejected the deal were labeled intransigent backwoodsmen and there was the insinuation that they were against the idea of peace.

Of course peace comes in many guises; it can, for example, be the peace that follows an ignoble surrender to an enemy. Conflict may finish but what price has been paid? Is peace at any price an ideal worth pursuing? If accommodating the wish list of Irish terrorists is the key to peace, why wait thirty years and three thousand deaths before accepting it? Could peace not have been instantly won back in 1969 when the IRA commenced its' killing campaign?

Political events in Northern Ireland between 1997 and 2007 have substantially redefined what unionism stands for and just as importantly, what it stands against. There are now two variants within unionism: the greater one which embraces the Belfast Agreement/Good Friday Agreement and its bastard scion the St. Andrews Accord, and another smaller group which comprehensively rejects both. During these years, I have found myself inextricably linked with the latter group, and, after years of having pro-Agreement apologists pumping out their self-serving propaganda on what is called a peace process, it seems timely to voice the views of those opposed to power-sharing with terrorists, no matter how offensive this is to the peace processors within the political establishment.

It's not as if the mainstream media has ever been particularly sympathetic towards those people in Northern Ireland who seek to retain their British identity and remain in a political union with Great Britain. Any vestige of such understanding vanishes like snow of a ditch when it becomes apparent that not only is one pro-British and pro-monarchist but also opposed to the much vaunted peace process. Pride in being British is a concept that many within the media and political elite appear to struggle to relate to in any significant degree.

In fact over the time that Labour has sat in power, it seems that those groups which despise British values and which work to subvert the British State gain far greater media sympathy and understanding. Blow up a train on the London Underground and there will be a queue of liberal apologists wanting to blame British foreign policy; try and stop an IRA bomber from blowing up innocents in Northern Ireland and there will be a queue of quislings agreeing that there must be an enquiry into state brutality. In the United Kingdom, the will to fight and defeat terrorism has become increasingly eroded as the government seeks to find less confrontational ways to ensure the safety of its citizens.

That's one reason why the Northern Ireland peace process carries lessons that should resonate across the world and which are directly relevant to the much broader war on terror. Northern Ireland shows what happens when appeasement of terror becomes first sanitised and then institutionalised. It demonstrates how terrorists can achieve victory with just the mere threat of violence. It graphically illustrates the fragility of modern democracy and how easily it can become corrupted whilst the majority of the community is made to feel content. Above all, it makes clear that democracy and terrorism cannot be combined and a civilised and moral society produced.

Where does unionism find itself in 2008? What purpose has it in this 21st century, against a geo-political topography in which globalisation has made national barriers less and less relevant? What is the contemporary essence of unionism and in what way has the peace process contributed towards this? Who speaks for unionists and what are they saying? Is devolution the best defence unionism can secure, or is it a poisoned chalice that will finish off the union? Could a form of hybrid unionism survive in a united Ireland? Did the Belfast Agreement/Good Friday Agreement strengthen or weaken the union? Does power-sharing with terrorists assist the unionist cause? Would unionists be better off to abandon their political creed now, cut a deal and embrace Irish unity from a position of relative strength? Have the wishes of ordinary unionists been sold out by a weak-willed and compromised political elite whose only apparent function has been to secure the benefits of power, privilege and patronage for itself and to hell with the consequences for the country? Do ordinary unionists place a real value on their British citizenship, or is it an ephemeral extra to be traded in for the best alternative deal?

The starting point in this discussion has to be the momentous decision taken by the Ulster Unionist Party in September 1997 to enter a political process set up and carefully calibrated by the British and Irish governments. This decision broke several unionist taboos. It implicitly accepted that the Irish government could play a central role in directing political discussions concerning an internal part of the United Kingdom. It conceded direct political discussion with various sets of terrorists, primarily the Irish Republican Army (IRA), but with the Ulster Volunteer Force (UVF) and Ulster Defence Association (UDA) as attendant sideshows. Worse still, it failed to appreciate that these were not in any normal sense negotiations since the outcome was already predetermined by the two sovereign governments and led inexorably to the political deal called the Belfast Agreement aka the Good Friday Agreement. Between that date in 1997 and the 8th May 2007, unionism has gone through tumultuous change. It's been a decade of decayed unionism.

How could such a change have taken place, and why have all elected unionist leaders concluded that there is no alternative but accepting that power-sharing with the IRA's front men in Sinn Fein is the only way forward?

Therein lies the tale, and lies have been telling the tale ever since 1997. For slightly more than a decade, the people of Northern Ireland have been exposed to a 24/7 media news cycle which has relentlessly extolled the virtues of the peace process as if it were

Holy Writ, beyond even the mildest criticism. But what exactly has the peace process been about?

First and foremost, the peace process has never been about peace. Understanding this point is critical, because the impression that peace has been the driver of the political developments experienced in Northern Ireland has sustained the grand illusion conjured up by those seeking to disguise a tatty and immoral appeasement of western Europe's largest and most vicious terrorist group, the Irish Republican Army (IRA). To be clear, the purpose of the peace process has been to appease IRA terrorism and to sacrifice the wishes of the peaceful, law-abiding majority in Northern Ireland who seek to maintain their British identity.

The reality is that the form of peace being sold in Northern Ireland is no different in substance to that Britain purchased in 1938 when the then UK Prime Minister, Neville Chamberlain, also commenced a short-lived but much vaunted peace process with Mr. Hitler. The same craven instincts that prevailed then within the British political establishment have also directed events in Northern Ireland over the past decade. The same hollow cheers that accompanied the appeasement of Nazi Germany can also be found in the cheers of those political knaves who supported the appeasement of the IRA and the other terror groups found in Northern Ireland.

The key driver of this appeasement revolved around an urgent need to buy off the IRA from committing any further bombing spectaculars in the commercial heart of England, such as that which occurred on the 24th April 1993 in the City of London and again in Manchester on 15th June 1996. The massive costs of these bombings severely hurt the financial interests of the UK government, and it became critical to find a way to stop any further such explosions. The IRA had accidentally stumbled across a key weakness within the British establishment, and this was evidenced in the news that the cost of the 1992 bombing of the Baltic Exchange in London was said to have been greater than all the damages paid out in Northern Ireland for death, personal injury and property between 1969 and 1992. Put simply, it was considered cheaper to buy off the IRA than to keep fighting them.

The deal was a very simple one: in exchange for the IRA graciously ceasing to bomb the British mainland, the UK government would work hand in glove with the Irish government to deliver gradualised Irish unity. Shamefully, the British government had permitted itself to become a covert persuader for Irish unity. In many ways, this is the tale of a State turning against its own people, or at least the section of them whose loyalty was unwanted and whose continued presence in the nation was deemed too expensive.

It was clear to all concerned that Northern Ireland's unionist majority was not interested in exchanging their British passports for Irish ones. Even after decades of bombings and shootings, the pro-union people were still determined to remain British. Any sudden constitutional change would most likely result in some form of unionist uprising, as the majority wishes were sacrificed to accommodate a violent minority. So a more cunning plan was required, one which introduced g-r-a-d-u-a-l-i-s-m as the central engine of political change. This was the undeniable genius behind political developments going forward from this time. Given enough time, unionist politicians would prove themselves capable of accepting all kinds of changes to their position: a self-confessed IRA commander as Education Minister, the destruction of the force of law in the shape of the Royal Ulster Constabulary (RUC), even the release of convicted murderers. All this was to become possible, but first unionist political acquiescence had to be obtained and every resource was directed to achieve this end.

The Belfast Agreement/Good Friday Agreement provided the basis for this. After all, it was politically advantageous for some within unionism to sign up for what was presented to the world as peace. Those who embraced the deal were hailed as politicians with vision, doves of peace, politicians big enough to accept compromise. Yet perhaps the most curious aspect to the Belfast Agreement/Good Friday Agreement is that whilst republicans proclaimed it accelerated their aim of a united Ireland, some unionists declared that it had secured the union. Quite clearly both points of view could not be simultaneously correct, but, thanks to an unprecedented propaganda blitz driven by a newly elected British Labour government, a slim majority of unionist voters actually turned out at the poll and endorsed this incredulous position.

Nobel Peace Prizes were swiftly dished out to those at the heart of the deal. Ulster Unionist leader David Trimble even got praised by Bono from U2. If the sainted Bono was for it, who could be against it? The realpolitik at work here was the calculated consideration that if the Ulster Unionist Party said this was the right thing to do, and given that it was the largest party within unionism at this time, then a substantial part of the electorate would choose to believe what it was being told and follow this judgement call.

Let me be clear. I firmly believe that unionism suffered a potentially terminal blow on the day that the people of Northern Ireland, including a slim majority of unionists, voted YES to a political agreement specifically designed to bring about the gradualised destruction of the Union. It doesn't matter why they voted as they did, nor does it matter that many subsequently felt cheated, the fact is that this vote triggered a series of seismic events, some of which are still unfolding, and these place the future of the Union in serious doubt.

The media portrayed the result of the 1998 referendum as a victory for peace. It was euphoric in how it presented the images following the referendum vote and any sense of media neutrality vanished.

With a soundtrack of Van Morrison singing that there would be more *"Days like this"* if only the people said "Yes" to what was on offer, Goethe's Faust might have rushed into agreeing to the deal. After all, what was there to lose?

One of the most distinguishing aspects of this referendum was that the result could not be challenged or changed in the future. The architects of the Belfast Agreement/Good Friday Agreement were hell-bent to make sure that once the people had spoken they would never speak again! In effect, it became written in tablets of stone, non-reversible, a one-way vote. Of course in a democracy, people are entitled to change their minds from time to time and to reverse some things that they no longer like. But that was clearly not the case with this one-way referendum.

The media were playing an active role in the process and not just in reporting it. This created a tremendous difficulty for those opposed to the Belfast Agreement/Good Friday Agreement since they were constantly portrayed as begrudgers, the enemies of peace. Whenever serious doubts were voiced about what was on offer, the inevitable question posed back was ...but what is your alternative? This is a faux question since it implies that compromise with terrorists is a valid course of action in a civilised democracy. It isn't. It also suggests that opening up the prison gates and releasing convicted mass murderers is an equitable course of action. It's not. Finally, and most perversely of all, it seeks to suggest that any alternative proposition put forward has to win the support of blood thirsty terrorists. It doesn't. Why is it that the tender mercies of brutal killers matter most? Those who asked what is the alternative to the peace process left out the words *"acceptable to the terrorists."* Of course, to add these would expose the inherent moral bankruptcy of the peace processors. And that would never do.

Whenever unionists argued that the alternative to releasing convicted murderers was to keep them in prison, this was met with media incomprehension and dismay. Whenever it was suggested that the alternative to allowing terrorists to sit in government was to vigorously keep them out of power, this was also dismissed as unhelpful and lacking vision. The brutal truth is that the agenda being pursued implied that it was normal to turn the conventions of democracy on their head, and that it was brave and decent to set the rule of law to one side and admirable to punish the force of law, the Royal Ulster Constabulary. At every turn, it was argued that there was no alternative to that being implemented. Stalin had used much the same technique many years earlier. In truth, the 1998 Belfast Agreement/Good Friday Agreement reeked of Orwell's 1984, with words coming to mean the opposite of what was said. There was no peace, but there was plenty of appeasement.

I recall speaking with fellow unionists back then, and they were clearly divided into two camps. There were those who had obviously been softened up by years of terrorism and a lying British government. They felt that although it was a risk to swallow the Belfast Agreement/Good Friday Agreement, it was still a risk worth taking. *"Sure, what have we got to lose?"* they asked. They did not really believe that the RUC was about to be sacrificed, nor did they think that IRA/Sinn Fein would soon enter government even though it had neither disbanded nor disarmed. UK Prime Minister, Tony Blair, produced handwritten promises which indicated that these things would not happen; but then again constructive ambiguity was the name of the peace process game; and some of those persuaded to support the process in 1998 lived to regret it in the years ahead. Of course it was far too late by then.

From the moment a section of unionists accepted the terms of the Belfast Agreement/Good Friday Agreement, those who opposed it were branded heretics. It was obvious even back in 1998 that a substantial body of unionist opinion did not buy into the process, but their reservations were swept aside because the majority thought otherwise. (Majoritarianism seemed acceptable in some conditions, obviously.) The media focus has always been on those who went along with the prevailing political wind, but there has been less attention devoted to the consequences of this for unionism. Momentum forward was considered progress in itself, although if one were standing at a cliff-edge, would this still be considered a good thing?

For any section of unionism to accept a political process which rewarded terrorists was a hammer blow to the integrity of their position. For some unionists to align themselves with terror groups was equally repellent, yet that is exactly what happened from 1997 onwards. In the run up to the Belfast Agreement/Good Friday Agreement, the government facilitated the creation of two small unionist parties: the Progressive Unionist Party (PUP) and the Ulster Democratic Party (UDP). Both parties were political fronts for loyalist terrorism and their elevation was encouraged in order that the government could ensure all the major terror gangs were in the same room bartering for as much as they could get.

The impact of these mutant unionists at the polls was minimal with the electorate mostly refusing to lend such monstrosities a vote. However, the PUP managed to pick up a few seats in Belfast and the Ulster Unionist Party leadership came to rely on these votes. The iconic image of David Trimble leading his UUP team into the Assembly flanked by PUP and UDP delegates summed up just how degraded this section of unionism had already become. They felt no shame in relying on the support of the political representatives of gangsters and thugs. In the new peace process era, those politicians who cavorted with paramilitary proxies were the new heroes, whilst those who condemned any association with such terror warlords were portrayed as villains.

The Ulster Unionist Party had a certain reputation as being the more moderate and middle of the road party within unionism.

Whether this was deserved or not is a different matter, but it does seem all the more remarkable that this was the section of unionism to first cave in to the idea that power-sharing with those who sought to end the union was a good idea. Indeed given the IRA's record of murdering UUP politicians and bombing its headquarters, it is a testament to the skill of those peace processors such as US Senator George Mitchell that they were able to convince Mr. Trimble and his colleagues to support a process which clearly rewarded the IRA and punished those who upheld the law.

When the Executive of the Assembly sat in November 1999, Martin McGuinness, a self-confessed senior IRA terrorist assumed the role of Minister for Education. This created a collective gasp across unionism, but the UUP leadership appeared content with this, assuring their electorate that there was nothing to fear. This became a familiar Ulster Unionist ploy, asserting that all would be well, that they alone fully understood the complexity of the process they were participating within, and then when events proved them completely wrong, there would be a shrug before moving on to the next debacle. When McGuinness immediately used his position to initiate a process aimed at bringing about the demise of academic-based selection and thus the de facto destruction of the grammar school system, UUP voices became mute once more.

Criticism is not directed solely at the UUP. The next ten years would see the Democratic Unionist Party (DUP) also follow in the same steps and eventually conclude that Mr. McGuinness was a suitable partner in government. Polls would be produced to show that most of unionism grass roots endorsed such a stance. In fact, throughout the peace process years, convenient polls became a favoured mechanism used by the government to suggest that progress was being made. There were even newspaper polls showing that the Ulster Unionist Party would perform well in the General Election of 2005, just before it was virtually annihilated at the ballot box poll. Lies, damned lies, and polling statistics!

In a peace process land, nothing is ever quite as it appears. The government controls most of the strings, and the logic of Humpty Dumpty prevails.

> **"When I use a word", Humpty Dumpty said, in a rather scornful tone, "it means just what I choose it to mean, neither more nor less." "The question is", said Alice, "whether you can make words mean so many different things." "The question is," said Humpty Dumpty, "which is to be master - that's all"**

And indeed, that is all that matters. Words have been bent and twisted out of all shape over the past ten years. Terrorists are presented as victims; the lawless are portrayed as our best chance for peace. It was the former Conservative Prime Minister, John Major, who declared that only the men of violence could bring about a lasting peace. That's akin to saying that only a wife beater can bring domestic harmony. True in one way, but not something any decent person could tolerate. But decency has had nothing to do with the Northern Ireland political process for decades. Lies were redefined as constructive ambiguity to smirks all round, and the unsung heroes of the process were a couple of convicted mass murderers called Michael (Stone) and Johnny (Adair), if Secretary of State Mo Mowlam was to be believed.

Many euphemisms have been invented to try and get past the immorality of what has been carried out by our politicians. Every time a promise was broken, this was hailed as *"a risk for peace"* Every time an inconvenient truth was flagged up, we were told to forget all about it and *"leave the past behind and move forward"*. The vocabulary of the terrorists became employed by the media, and those who opposed the Belfast Agreement/Good Friday Agreement were categorised as *"rejectionists"*, a preferred IRA/Sinn Fein term.

During the long ten years between 1997 and 2007, the IRA killed at least 37 people. Paul Daly was sitting with his 11-year-old daughter in his car near the nationalist Unity Flats on May 4, 2001 when two gunmen approached and shot him dead. Michael Magee was recovering from a savage IRA punishment beating at his home in Downpatrick on June 11, 2001 when a masked gang broke in and shot him dead at point-blank range. Trevor Kells was a Protestant taxi driver who answered a call to Ardoyne on December 5, 2000 and was shot dead by two IRA gunmen. And whilst these murders were taking place, the likes of Gerry Adams and Martin McGuinness insisted that IRA guns were silent. This obvious republican lie was routinely parroted by the media and the peace processing class, even though it was obvious that IRA guns were far from silent. But in Humpty Dumpty land, such things don't matter.

What is less commonly understood is that the IRA was permitted to retain its illegal weapons to enforce justice mafia-style within the nationalist community. The State turned a blind eye to the violence that the IRA would inflict on those poor people unfortunate enough to cross it. The terms of the Belfast Agreement/Good Friday Agreement did not stop the IRA from murdering as it saw fit, it merely requested that Sinn Fein use such influence as it might have to stop this. The key part of the deal was to get the IRA to stop bombing the commercial heart of the UK and killing British soldiers, what it did to those within the Roman Catholic community who irritated it was summed up as internal housekeeping by NI Secretary of State, Mo Mowlam. As my then political colleague Conor Cruise O'Brien pointed out at the time:

"When the Secretary of State for Northern Ireland was questioned about what she meant by that nauseating euphemism, the sinister meaning of it became all too clear. In essence, internal housekeeping means that

paramilitary groups are now recognised by the British authorities as free to run the areas they choose to regard as their own in whatever ways they choose, subject to certain specified limitations. As long as they refrain from attacking British soldiers and the members of the RUC, or persons living in communities other than those as recognised as being within their jurisdiction, they can run their own territories just as they like. Mo Mowlam was defending her own decision not to treat a recent murder, which she acknowledged to have been committed by the IRA, as a breach of the IRA cease-fire. Rather the murder was covered by this novel doctrine of internal housekeeping"

It's not only a novel doctrine, but is also one without any discernible morality and yet it has been a central tenet of the peace process. Whatever happened to the sanctity of human life? Who cares when you're busy peace processing?

What has taken place in Northern Ireland has been hailed as a model template that can be used around the world to solve seemingly intractable conflict. It is seen by some as Tony Blair's most significant political success and those local politicians, who have gone along with it, together with the terrorists it has rewarded, are now portrayed as statesmen.

On July 16th 2007 the First Minister of the Northern Ireland Assembly, a beaming Dr Ian Paisley stood beside a smiling Martin McGuinness on the marbled steps of the Stormont Parliament building and declared *"Peace, perfect Peace."* But what sort of peace is it that places terror warlords in positions of major political influence? It's time to lift the cover once and for all off the obscenity that is passed off as a peace and to expose the total depravity that lies at the heart of this corrupting process.

TRUST

It is said that the secret of success is sincerity. Once you can fake that, you've got it made. Back in May 2000, Prime Minister Tony Blair was demonstrating his mastery of this art by presenting his cast-iron promise to the Northern Ireland electorate that:

> **"I give my word, and I will keep it. There will be no fudge between democracy and terror. Only those who have given up violence for good can play a part in the democratic future of Northern Ireland."**

Cresting on a tsunami of media induced approval for his *"persistence"* with peace processing in Northern Ireland, Mr. Blair was portrayed as an honest-broker, the man that unionists really could trust. But the pro-union people would have done well to reflect on the words of Lord Palmerston, the 19th century politician who observed;

> **"We have no eternal allies, and we have no perpetual enemies. Our interests are eternal and perpetual, and those interests it is our duty to follow."**

All Blair was doing when he came to power in 1997 was following these eternal and perpetual interests. It was nothing personal, of course, just taking care of business. When it came to matters of trust, Blair had already acquired a poor reputation for those who cared to look.

Back in 1998, he had traveled to Northern Ireland in order to stand in front of his very own hand-written pledges assuring the unionist electorate that it had really nothing to fear if it were to vote "Yes" in the looming referendum, because he would act as their personal guarantor to make certain that....

- **"Those who use or threaten violence to be excluded from the government of Northern Ireland"**

- **"Prisoners to be kept in prison unless violence is given up for good"**

Tragically, many unionists did trust him. Many saw him as "their" Prime Minister, even if no-one in the province had actually voted for him, and unionists tend to invest a lot of faith in the occupant of Number 10 Downing Street. He looked like and spoke like a *"pretty straight kind of guy"*, and so it was that just a few months later, in September 1998, that the first of hundreds of convicted terrorists strolled free from prison. Not that long afterwards, in 1999 Sinn Fein entered the government of Northern Ireland. The IRA remained intact and active, as did the UVF and UDA. Mr. Blair had betrayed the trust placed in him, and his promises had proven worthless.

In fairness, it had been like that from the beginning. When the wheels first threatened to come off the project as early as April 1998, Blair was forced to fly to Northern Ireland in order to calm the ruffled feathers of alarmed unionists. It was at this moment when he provided one of his most unintentionally hilarious sound-bites. Assuring waiting journalists that this was not a time for sound-bites, he added that he felt *"the hand of history"* on his shoulders.

During my short time in front-line politics, along with colleagues in the UKUP, I met with several of those who carried out the role of Northern Ireland Secretary of State. Mo Mowlam, Peter Mandelson, Paul Murphy and John Reid all held this high office of state and whilst they each had an individual style, the one thing that came across to me was that they were all absolutely devoted to ensuring that nothing, and no-one, would de-rail the *"peace process."* They would listen politely (in most cases) to our arguments when we insisted that it was morally wrong to negotiate with terrorists and that they were compromising the very standards of democracy. Then they would smile wearily and point out that this was all very well, but we all had to move forward if ever progress was going to be made, and that meant talking to those with whom they felt uncomfortable. In their case, I think they meant people like Robert McCartney and myself, not the terror warlords!

The important role of Secretary of State for Northern Ireland was spectacularly debased by those such as Mo Mowlam who made a virtue out of developing warm relationships with the proxies for the IRA, UVF and UDA. How on earth could any decent unionist place faith in such rancid hypocrites? Who in their right political mind would trust representatives of a government which was doing everything possible to cultivate friendships with some of the most wicked people in the country? Being loyal to a government which is venomously intent on betraying some of its' most loyal citizens is a very difficult position to sustain. Unionism by its very nature has tried to be loyal, and, whilst that loyalty is primarily placed in the Crown, the hard fact is that it is government where real power resides, and this has always been the *schwerpunkt* for unionism.

It's all very well for Irish nationalists to boast of their insurrection; after all they delight in their lack of loyalty to the British state. For decades this contempt for the state has won them plaudits from the international political elite. But unionists have found themselves in the impossible position of seeking to affirm their British credentials whilst dealing with a government, particularly in the shape of Labour, which has been committed to establishing a united Ireland. This inherent conflict has undeniably strengthened the drive for devolution and may be the reason why unionism has eventually morphed into Ulster nationalism.

Blaming unionist politicians for going down this road is perhaps a little unfair insofar as they had to deal with those at Westminster who cared little for the union and who continuously showed a callous disregard for the wishes of the pro-union people. Devolution was the one obvious route for unionists to try and gain a better level of control over their destiny, and the fact that both major unionist parties have been devoutly committed to achieving this did not go un-noticed by the British government. This lust to gain local power was perhaps natural, but the price tag which accompanied it was always going to be prohibitive to anyone who actually cared about the long-term survival of the union. In essence, the Blair government baited the prospect of devolution with constitutional poison. Those unionists who had previously baulked at sharing power with constitutional nationalists, such as the SDLP, were now faced with the very real prospect of sharing power with the IRA's proxies. All they had to do was close their eyes, lie back and think of Ulster.

Other political thinkers within unionism had advocated integration in the form of full administrative incorporation with Great Britain as a means of coping with an untrustworthy government. During the 1980's these people led a campaign for equal citizenship, arguing that main British political parties, such as the Labour and Conservative, should organise and stand for election in Northern

Ireland. Although Labour and Conservative parties said in 1988 that they would not organise in Northern Ireland, the Conservative Party was forced, by a vote at its annual conference in 1989, to begin campaigning in the region. It never really quite took off, however, and the Conservative vote amongst the Northern Ireland electorate has subsequently dwindled away.

Labour continues to refuse to organise in Northern Ireland, such is its contempt for the people of the province. The advent of the Labour regime in 1997 committed to devolution ensured that integration was not going to be part of the political agenda going forward. The primary problem with integration was that it might have proven successful as a means to secure the union since it would have provided the Conservative and Labour parties with interests in Northern Ireland. But they did not want such assets, and, therefore, to varying degrees, it has been rejected by both the major political parties in Great Britain who sought to keep Northern Ireland at a studied distance. Another real problem with it was that it would have limited political ambitions for local politicians so they too did not invest heavily in the theoretical notion.

As well as having to deal with a mendacious government, unionists have also had to find a way to deal with the power that this government wields over the media. It is said that you shouldn't believe everything that you read, but, when it comes to trusting the media in Northern Ireland, it would be better to say that you shouldn't believe anything that you read, or hear, or see. The courtier media embraced the peace process project from the start with an obscene relish and did everything possible to advance it.

A good example of this was the way in which the IRA's decision to allegedly decommission its' illegal terror arsenal in 2005 was hailed as being of truly historical proportions. Media coverage was certainly of hysterical proportions, but the truth remained that the Provo's alleged "act of completion" was invisible. There was no evidence of what had been decommissioned, no open inventory of what this supposedly constituted, and all that was provided was the assurances of two "independent" witnesses chosen by the IRA. Yet the media, those alleged independent minded fearless seekers of truth and justice, swallowed this IRA PR without so much as a moment's hesitation, and so it was the government agenda was advanced by the fourth estate in full-on compliance mode. This media induced jubilation created headlines around the world. It opened doors for IRA/Sinn Fein, but it also raised the question as to why so many within the international community were euphoric whilst many unionists remained decidedly underwhelmed? The media puzzled over this and seemed genuinely perplexed that the unionist community, which the IRA had invested so much time methodically butchering for more than three decades, had not spontaneously burst into the Hallelujah chorus and perhaps a reel from Riverdance at this new dawn.

In fact, rather than commit to its own demise, the IRA arrogantly stated that it would not disband its terror infra-structure. It also insisted that the illegal *Army Council* would remain intact. This determination to keep the command structure in place was treated as a mere inconvenient footnote as the blaze of contrived publicity displayed the terrorists in the most favourable light imaginable. And for those who still doubted the bona fides of murdering terrorists, there were always those two IRA approved *"independent witnesses"* whose word was to be taken on trust.

The media in Northern Ireland portrays itself as if it were a neutral reporter of political events, and yet, when BBC Northern Ireland's chief political editor, Stephen Grimason, left the corporation in 2001 to join the administration of the devolved government, it was presented as the most natural of career changes. It is my view that the media in general in Northern Ireland has not been an independent observer but an active participant, a fervent and subtle persuader in favour of government policy.

This was manifest on the day of the referendum when the news broke that the "Yes" lobby had won the day. Beaming reporters announced this news and made no attempt to hide their obvious glee at this allegedly happy news! One cannot of course be sure how they voted, but I suspect that there were few, if any, journalists within the Northern Ireland media who voted against the depravity of the Belfast Agreement/Good Friday Agreement. Perhaps there was more newsworthiness in reporting the views of the terrorist class, and certainly those political spokesmen for the terror groups tended to get a very easy ride from many, though not all, journalists.

Some basic questions were never asked by these allegedly intrepid seekers of truth; for example, the fiction was continually presented that Gerry Adams had nothing to do with the IRA. If he had nothing to do with the IRA, why was he afforded such prominence by sovereign governments? Who DID lead the IRA, precisely? Who was the man who directed this terror gang, who were his associates, where did they live, and what did they do during the daylight hours at least? It was the same with the UVF and UDA for that matter. The ludicrous notion was kept running that the political proxies were in no way directly connected to the actual terror groups, they just bumped into the balaclava brigade from time to time and provided political analysis to them. The media had a very important role to play in presenting a broad and balanced perspective on the developing political agenda, but it never stepped up to the plate. Instead it chose a role on the same side as the peace processors.

Whether it was TV, radio or print, the media took a pro-Agreement view and this was endlessly repeated throughout the period from 1997 to 2007. Reporters looked aghast when it was gently pointed out to them that the alternative to letting terrorists out of prison was to keep them in prison, and they were astonished when reminded that the IRA, UVF and UDA were a pack of murdering thugs. Trusting in balanced media coverage of political events was a complete non-starter, and yet it was the major provider of news for most of the people. The growth of the internet would slightly change this, but, for these critical years, there was unanimous approval from the chattering classes for the peace processing being carried out.

It strikes me that above all else, unionist politicians lack trust in themselves. At 8.45am on September 11th 2001, the IRA was effectively decommissioned as a result of Al Qaeda attacking the United States. Suddenly all terrorist groups of global outreach were faced with the reality that they either ceased their bombings and shootings or faced the wrath of an angry and dramatically energised American administration.

The Clintonian years of indulgence were now over, and the IRA had some serious decisions to make. In effect, it has spent the time since that dreadful day developing a strategy of wringing endless concessions from the craven UK government in exchange for publicly acknowledging the obvious: namely that its illegal armaments were as redundant as the reasons for using them. In 2005 all that happened was that the IRA decided to admit that it cannot use its own weapons. It agreed to do this on the basis that the British government allowed it to retain its toxic criminal empire (under new management, of course) and accept arrangements that would mean it could police its' own areas. It was an IRA cosmetic make-over in exchange for a British political roll-over.

IRA/Sinn Fein's strategy to enter government simultaneously both sides of the border took a major hit in the election held in the Republic of Ireland in May 2007. Instead of winning seats and catapulting itself into power, it was found with egg all over its face. This unforeseen failure in political strategy was put down to a woeful TV performance by Gerry Adams and voters actually reflecting on whether this party should be put in a position where it could actually exercise serious power. Unionists were delighted that Adams and his associates were now seen as untrustworthy by the southern electorate, and this was portrayed as a serious blow to the all-Ireland aspirations of IRA/Sinn Fein.

However this is to entirely underestimate Irish republicans. In Northern Ireland, Gerry Adams is the man with star charisma as far as many nationalists are concerned. There is no evidence to suggest that Adams' political fortunes north of the border will decline, and indeed the ongoing sanitisation of his party in Northern Ireland politics as it postures as a governing party may yet get it to the point where the softer edges of unionism could embrace it. (A poll in a newspaper in the summer of 2007 claimed that the majority of unionists believed that Martin McGuinness was doing a good job!)With reported income of almost £1 million in 2006, republicans have the financial clout to address the hurdles which derailed them in the Irish general election, and they will try and carefully re-calibrate the implementation of their strategy to correct this setback. Unionists who think that one electoral set-back has seen off the republican agenda are both forgetful and foolish in the extreme.

What is particularly degrading from a democrats' perspective is that the British government and the mainstream media were now doing the propagandising for this grotesque terrorist group. They presented the false impression that the IRA has chosen the path of peace and has finally decided to commit itself to democratic politics. They were mute about the fact that the IRA still retains its terror structure, and obfuscated the fact that the IRA has dramatically expanded its criminal empire culminating in the UK's biggest bank robbery in December of 2004. They ignored the fact that IRA hoods swagger around Northern Ireland considering themselves as beyond the reach of the law, the new untouchables.

In fact, these thugs believe that they ARE the law, and 2007 saw IRA/Sinn Fein join the Policing Board of Northern Ireland – the body to which the Chief Constable had to come and report. They would oversee the PSNI and make sure it delivered. Two of the three nominated IRA/Sinn Fein member's to this prestigious body possessed impressive CV's. One was a convicted IRA bomber (Martina Anderson), and the other was a convicted bank robber (Alex Maskey). Only in peace-process land, where decency had been banished, could the placement of such notorious individuals be hailed as a huge step forward. Once more unionists were being asked to place their trust in a Policing Board which contained those convicted of breaking the law. Astoundingly by the time this had happened, the two main unionist parties were quite prepared to sit around the table and discuss the future policing priorities of Northern Ireland with those who belonged to an organisation that had murdered hundreds of police officers and maimed many thousands more.

Considering the track record of the unionist political elite, the pro-union electorate would do well to place little trust in them. It seems that rather than try and advance the unionist case and risk head-on confrontation with government and the media, unionist politicians prefer to immediately start working on new ways to explain away their serial failure. This is a peculiar feature of unionism; it's as if the start point is always behind the political ball; and from there on in it's just a question of thinking up good reasons why there is no success. This is true of the Ulster Unionists and the Democratic Unionists. There are so many examples of this, and none of them offer any level of confidence to a thinking electorate.

It was the Ulster Unionist Party, under the leadership of David Trimble, which coined the term *"constructive ambiguity."* Such a euphemism for cloaking true intentions may win the applause of those sophisticates within the political elite but must horrify decent people who turn out to vote for specific policies. It was the UUP that declared that "the RUC is safe". The RUC was axed. It was the UUP that declared it would not engage in talks with IRA/Sinn Fein until decommissioning had commenced. Yet it sat in government with IRA/Sinn Fein and they decommissioned not even a bullet. It was the UUP that declared that all IRA decommissioning had to be completed by June 2001. It did not happen by this date. Time after time, the hopes of the ordinary person were smashed, not just by Irish republicans, but by their unionist leaders who huffed and puffed and then did nothing.

The DUP has proven to be equally untrustworthy. Dr. Paisley made it clear on July 12th 2006 that it would only be *"over his dead body"* that IRA/Sinn Fein would enter government. Since he gave every impression of being still alive when he voluntarily entered government with IRA/Sinn Fein under a year later, in May 2007, one can only presume that his boastings were as hollow as his shouts of *"Never, Never, Never"* to the interference of the Irish government in the affairs of Northern Ireland. He has, of course, become a much welcomed visitor to the office of the Irish Prime Minister.

It was Dr. Paisley's deputy, Peter Robinson, who assured unionists that it could take *"up to a generation"* for republicans to become fit for government. Instead, it only took a few months. Time flies when you're being glum. The pattern amongst this political class is always the same; make a bold claim and then when it becomes apparent that it will not happen, shrug the shoulders and make it clear that things could have been a lot worse had the claim not been made in the first place!

Canvassing on the doorstep during various election campaigns, the thing that struck me most was the huge tribalism that characterises the unionist electorate. They suffer from the *"Judean Popular front"* syndrome insofar as, if there was one thing that UUP voters hated more than republicans, it was the DUP! And the feeling appeared reciprocal, with DUP supporters equally vehement in their dislike of the UUP. Trying to explain that neither party could be entirely relied upon to do what they said carried little weight, as loyalty to the given tribe trumped all reason. For this reason, I see no prospect for another successful unionist party emerging in the foreseeable future.

At time of writing, there is media speculation that a new *"traditional"* unionist party may emerge, and the former DUP MEP, Jim Allister, could be a possible leader for the disaffected. Whilst I wish all principled unionists well, my own experience suggests that any new party will struggle to make a major impact in the long term. That said, disgruntled voters are always capable of expressing their anger by providing a mandate to those who highlight the arrogance and decadence of the political unionist establishment.

One of the side effects of the peace process years, and which its' advocates remain studiously mute about, is that it has actually deepened polarisation in society; with the differing sides becoming more suspicious of each other, marking out more of their *"own"* territory, choosing to live apart from one and other.

One particular study by Dr. Gillian Robinson, based on data from the Northern Ireland Life and Times survey, showed that the proportion of people believing that relations between Catholics and Protestants are *"better now than five years ago"* fell from 50 percent in 1998 to 28 percent in 2001. This pessimism was markedly greater among Protestants than Catholics. In other words, unionist voters appeared to believe that they were losing out, but, strangely, they continued to place their trust in parties that betrayed it! One only has to view the new housing estates being built for new generations of families to observe that they are mostly made up with either one side or the other. The notion that the peace processing has united the people is damned by the very demographics of where people choose to live.

Those who can be sufficiently motivated to go out and vote (and, in unionist terms, this number sadly diminishes at each election) seem driven by fear as much as anything else. The DUP in particular regularly produces the bogey-man of *"republicans becoming the biggest party"* in order to catch those who may waiver in casting their vote. In other words, it is not who you vote for, it is who you vote against.

Unionist manifestos positively gleam with shiny new promises aimed at enticing the trusting voter. We've had the *"Time for a Fair Deal"* manifesto from the DUP in 2003, in which they hilariously promised to stop IRA/Sinn Fein getting permanently into government. They also raised the spectre that Gerry Adams could become Deputy First Minister if unionists were not careful for whom they voted. However, it turned out to be Martin McGuinness that got the gig so no pressure there! They followed this up in 2005 with *"Leadership that's working"*, which contained the classic comedy line that voters should support them because…

> **"…the unionist community does not want to go back to the bad old days when the UUP was in charge and daily conceded to Sinn Fein/IRA."**

Just a few years later, the DUP was "in charge" together with IRA/Sinn Fein. Plus ca change?

Not to be outdone when it came to peddling fantasies for the voters, the Ulster Unionist Party pledged in 2003 that it would work tirelessly to bring about the end of all paramilitarism, loyalist and republican. The slight problem with this was that they had said the same thing back in 1998, and then decided that, once *"in charge"*, they would meekly accept paramilitary proxies as their partners in power and would work alongside paramilitary linked political parties! Who would trust them when they had a clear record of broken promises? They found out a few years later, in 2005, when they even had the nerve to promise the electorate that they would "fight" for fair rates and oppose any unfair water tax. The difficulty here was that the Ulster Unionist Party had played a key role instigating a process back in May 2003 that directly led to the very rates increases it now sought to fight against!

It doesn't matter which unionist party gets to play at being *"in charge"*, the truth is that neither can be trusted to stick to what it promises. Instead of giving these unionist politicians the keys to the city, it might have been better for the electorate to change the lock, but those who choose to vote seem prepared to trust those who have comprehensively proven they are untrustworthy.

THE WAY OF THE LEMMING

The Ulster Unionist Party has been central to the changes that have taken place over the past decade, and it is fair to say that the David Trimble leadership years will be looked back upon as amongst the most critical in determining the fate of unionism. The impact this party has had on the fortunes of Northern Ireland since 1997 has been pivotal, and it is worth understanding how a party once led by Lord Carson ended up looking like it was run by comedian Frank Carson.

Ulster unionism should have been my natural political home. After all, the idea of a pluralist political party that sought to bring about a decent and prosperous Northern Ireland for all of the people is very appealing; and many in the Ulster Unionist Party will insist that this is the situation with their party; but I'm afraid that the truth here is uglier than the fiction.

Having been born in the Quaker-built village of Bessbrook, an Ulster unionist political fortress in the republican wilderness of south Armagh, I rather identified with the Ulster Unionist Party (UUP) as the natural party of the union. Later I became aware of Dr. Ian Paisley starting up his party, but he was a "maverick" back in those days with little local support. (Of course, the good Doctor has subsequently come to view "mavericks" as a most undesirable political species, but back then things were rather different.)

Whilst my family was entirely non-party political, I did pick up on the fact that those public figures that represented the UUP were a few steps up the social ladder from working class people, and this "Big House" dimension did not impress me in the least. As I grew older, I came to view the Ulster Unionists as a group who firstly looked after their own and who were riddled with class snobbery. In many ways, it seemed to me, the party had been dipped in political aspic circa 1921 and had yet to move on. I had no interest in the UUP, although I did attend primary school in Bessbrook with the amiable Danny Kennedy, who was to become deputy leader of the party many years later!

In the spirit of balance, however, I also must say that I think the UUP had tried to defend the union to the best of its (limited) ability, and, indeed, it certainly had attracted the unwelcome attention of the IRA for its bother. As a child back in 1972, I can remember the assassination attempt on Ulster Unionist MP, John Taylor, by Irish republicans in Armagh. It happened nearby the swimming pool that I had visited but an hour or so beforehand; fortunately Mr. Taylor survived, but the IRA lodged five bullets in his skull.

When I was living as a student in Belfast in 1981, I recall the brutal slaying of the Ulster Unionist MP, Reverend Robert Bradford, gunned down at a local community centre. I also remember the vicious killing in 1983 of rising Ulster Unionist star, Edgar Graham, at Queen's University in Belfast. Wiping out intelligent Ulster Unionists seemed very much part of the IRA game plan in those dark days, and one would have thought that, having experienced such horror first-hand, the UUP could be relied upon not to compromise with such bloodthirsty gangsters. How wrong can you be?

Moving forward to the mid-90's, James Molyneaux was coming to the end of his period as leader of the party. There was significant dissent within the ranks of the UUP at his failure to achieve anything of value, and, whilst he may have been seen as a "safe pair of hands" by some, the problem was that those hands were not so much waving as slowly drowning!

I followed the leadership election contest to replace him with some interest. David Trimble was hardly the establishment figure expected to win, and I recall the local media predictably speculating that it would be one of his rival candidates, Ken Maginnis or John Taylor, that would more than likely win the day. But in the final analysis, Trimble came out clearly on top, handsomely beating John Taylor in the run-off. I was pleased about this result since Trimble was also my local MP in Upper Bann. His role in the Drumcree Parade stand-off at Portadown in the July of 1995, and the accompanying elevation in public profile that this had afforded him, undoubtedly had some impact on his electoral fortunes, and I suppose he was seen as a bit of a "right-wing" unionist back then. Appearances, of course, can be very deceiving! Trimble became leader on 8th September 1995 and it seemed to me that a new era was dawning. This was indeed the case, but how disastrous it would prove for the UUP!

Almost one year after David Trimble became leader, I met with him at the UUP headquarters in Glengall Street, Belfast. This was just after I had become chairman of the BPPU (Business and Professional People for the Union), and I led a delegation to meet Mr. Trimble. It proved to be a fiery encounter and we were all surprised at just how easily David Trimble lost his temper. My initial impression of being ushered into the UUP offices was the deferential tone that staff used to refer to the "The Leader". I have never liked inappropriate formality and thought the atmosphere strange and very old fashioned. It felt more like a museum than the headquarters of a modern political party and, come to think of it, I thought I caught sight of a few dinosaurs scuttling through the corridors of non-power!

The discussion was all about trying to understand the Ulster Unionist strategy with regard to the developing political process. UUP relations with the Irish government were to prove a tricky area for this discussion. Trimble was asked by one of my colleagues if he would engage in direct talks with the Irish government. He said that of course he would. This created a hostile response from my colleague, who felt that there should be no dialogue with a government that held a territorial claim to Northern Ireland. Both points of view were fair enough, but David Trimble went red in the face, and I thought he was going to reach out and throttle the offending questioner! He thumped the table and asked, "*How dare*" he be questioned on how he would operate "*his*" policy towards the Irish government. We felt this was an over-the-top reaction, and a sour atmosphere pervaded the rest of the meeting. If things had started badly with Mr. Trimble, they were to go quickly downhill!

One of the best descriptions I ever heard about David Trimble came from UK Unionist leader Robert McCartney, who said that Mr. Trimble combined the most dangerous aspects of a political personality: a highly developed mind but with no fixed bottom line. David Trimble projected the idea that he knew best, but intelligence without acumen is of little benefit in politics, and the years to come would cruelly expose the UUP leader's political shortcomings.

Suspicions about Mr. Trimble's flawed judgement appeared confirmed in September of the following year, 1997, when, despite advice offered, he entered a government-controlled talks process with IRA/Sinn Fein. This created outrage in the broader unionist community, many of whom were disgusted at this new tack he was taking, since it clearly meant that he would be negotiating with IRA/Sinn Fein, albeit indirectly.

Equally repellent was the link up between the UUP and two very minor, allegedly unionist parties – the Progressive Unionist Party (PUP) and the Ulster Democratic Party (UDP). These two parties were political fronts for the terror groups: the UVF and the UDA. Both these groups had carried out horrendous acts of terror during the previous decades, and to see the so-called "Natural Party of Government", as the UUP liked to portray itself, parlaying with the UDA and UVF mouthpieces was profoundly revolting. That said, the media lavished praise on the UUP for taking this "*risk for peace*"!

Some within Irish republicanism suggest that unionism is hypocritical for not condemning loyalist terrorists whilst damning the IRA, but the fact of the matter is that the image of the David Trimble-led Ulster Unionists flanked by the UDA and UVF political proxies nauseated many within unionism. Republicans also praised Trimble's entry into the talks process with these loyalist versions of IRA/Sinn Fein, so exposing their own hypocrisy. Having a terrorist about the place, so to speak, was the main objection for many within the pro-union community for what was done in their name.

The following Easter, in 1998, Mr. Trimble did that which many feared and committed his party to a sordid deal with IRA/Sinn Fein. All along he had been warned that the outcome of the talks he was involved in was already predetermined. Mr. Trimble was told that it was all about conflict resolution between the British government and the IRA. The former wanted to buy off the latter, and the price being asked by the IRA was a process of gradualised Irish unification. Now, of course, the UK government could not impose this unilaterally upon the people of Northern Ireland, so it needed to ensure that some gullible unionists participated in faux negotiations to give the cover required, and this is where Mr. Trimble's reckless and misplaced confidence in his own ability to negotiate was to play such a major and disastrous role.

The Ulster Unionists came out of the negotiations claiming that the union was secured; that the Irish government's ludicrous claims to Northern Ireland in Articles 1 &2 of the Irish Constitution had been removed; that the RUC was safe; and that they had got the surety that the IRA would decommission all of its' illegal weapons. This was all pure fantasy but it was presented by the media as if these were incontrovertible facts!

In fact, the reality was that the 1920 Government of Ireland Act – the Act which created Northern Ireland -- was repealed; the Irish government had exchanged its worthless territorial claims in Articles 1 &2 for an internationally recognised claim to ALL of the people of Northern Ireland; the RUC's demise was ensured; hundreds of convicted terrorists were allowed to walk free; the embryonic and unaccountable all-Ireland bodies were established; and the IRA was not tied down to decommission so much as one bullet. However, such was the unprecedented media spin that, even though the Ulster Unionist Party had made a calamitous misjudgement, it was nonetheless hailed as an unprecedented triumph. David Trimble, along with SDLP leader John Hume, was awarded a Nobel Peace Prize for his *progressiveness.* In a way, it was indeed a triumph – but a triumph for the skilful strategy of Irish republicans and the mendacity of the UK and Irish government mandarins who drafted the detail of what was "agreed".

It was obvious to anyone with insight that the Ulster Unionist negotiators lacked the professional skills required to get themselves a good deal, and their boastful claims would be ruthlessly exposed over the next eight years. This would cause a self-implosion in their party and see it virtually wiped off the map. The UUP high-water mark was in the immediate aftermath of this deal, when it captured 28 seats of the 108 in the Assembly Election of June 1998, making it the biggest political party present. At that time, it also had 10 Members of Parliament and an MEP. At local council level, the UUP held 185 seats, and so the claim to be the "natural party of government" still seemed defensible - though that was about to crash and burn. By embracing the Belfast Agreement/ Good Friday Agreement, the UUP embraced its own demise, but no one would hear of this in 1998.

It was towards the end of 1999 that the flawed judgement of David Trimble was to be most famously exposed. Having narrowly won the latest in what was to be a series of "Executive Meetings" (with only the tell tale clink of Zimmerframes giving an indication of the age profile of those who actually composed this "elite all-powerful executive"), the Upper Bann MP determined that he would go back in power with the IRA's front men.

"We have done our bit. Mr. Adams, it is over to you. We have jumped, you follow!"

This is the political acumen of an enthusiastic lemming. Trimble leapt into the abyss but Adams shrewdly decided not to follow! After plummeting downwards for three months over the political cliff, David Trimble was forced to pull the parachute cord and get out of continued government with IRA/Sinn Fein. This led to the suspension of the executive and political progress in Northern Ireland was frozen! The blame for this was directed towards the Ulster Unionists though in all fairness it was republicans who were causing all the problems.

35

By May 2000, Mr. Trimble had bounced back again into government with IRA/Sinn Fein after a complicated sequence of statements and deals that led to the IRA allegedly opening up some of its arms dumps for "independent" inspection. Of course, no one knew what was inspected, where it was inspected, or even how it was inspected! The hopelessness of Trimble's position becomes evident when one remembers that the political deal he had signed up to in 1998 was supposed to have led to the complete decommissioning of the IRA arsenal by June 2001. But not even one bullet had been publicly handed over by this date.

David Trimble's political capital had been severely eroded by the IRA's prevarication, but the media preferred not to dwell on that detail. They needed their man kept in place, and the next few years would be characterised by the continued eulogising of the "statesman-like" Trimble and the demonisation of those who opposed the Agreement, such as the vehemently anti-Agreement Dr. Paisley.

My next meeting with David Trimble was after he had assumed the position of First Minister of the Northern Ireland Assembly. Bob McCartney and I met with him at his office in Stormont. David Trimble was accompanied in this meeting by the UUP chief whip, Jim Wilson, and it was a very strange meeting. Bob was on his best behaviour, and Trimble himself was in conversational form, though with an undeniable (and again entirely misplaced) sense of his once again having out-witted "the Shinners" (IRA/Sinn Fein). But throughout the meeting, JimWilson never spoke, never even looked at us, but instead played with a small piece of silver paper he had rolled up in a little ball. He seemed pre-occupied with this. We got nowhere with Trimble, as expected, but left having at least exchanged pleasantries and shaken hands. On the way along the corridor from the First Minister's office, we looked at each other and asked the same question "*What on earth was Wilson doing with that silver paper ball?*" I concluded that perhaps he was pretending we weren't even worthy of a glance. Either that or he maybe he was in the early stage of constructing a tinfoil hat! It was a weird experience.

From that point on, I lost all patience with the UUP and could see they were inept beyond repair. That said, I remained friendly with a number of the younger and brighter Ulster Unionists such Peter Weir and Simon Hamilton. In the years ahead they would bail out of the crumbling UUP and join the DUP. Haemorrhaging young political talent was to be another direct consequence of the Trimble era. Losing such bright people was a terrible price to pay for indulging a leader who did not know in what political direction he was traveling.

In my local area in Upper Bann, I enjoyed jousting with the local UUP representatives through the pages of the local press. Now, in retrospect, this may have been an error since I am regularly told that no-one likes to see one unionist attack another. However, when the actions of that other unionist are so profoundly wrong, what can one do other than call it as you see it?

The UUP in Upper Bann – David Trimble apart – were in essence a comedy act. George Savage is my neighbour and also a prominent figure in the UUP. Indeed, he had been influential in helping David Trimble advance in the Upper Bann area within the party. (Trimble lived outside his constituency.) Mr. Savage had been elected to the Assembly on David Trimble's transfer votes in 1998. Now, even his best friends would accept that George is perhaps not a silver tongued cavalier. He is a farmer, and whilst I have absolute confidence in his ability to discern all bovine matters, when it comes to discussing constitutional complexities and dealing with the Machiavellian political traps laid by government, it's perhaps best to assume this was not his strongest area.

I had challenged any of the local Ulster Unionist MLA's to a public debate, anywhere, anytime. The intrepid George finally faced me at a local hall at a meeting hosted by the Loyal Orders. I fully prepared my speech and arrived all set for a verbal joust. I was quite happy for George to give his speech first, and then I would reply. The thing is that it wasn't really a speech that he made. It had no obvious start, lacked a middle section, and I think no one was sure when it had ended. Stunned, I put my speech away into my jacket pocket and ad-libbed because I felt sorry for him. I appreciated that not all political representatives were Premier League material, but this was decidedly Non-League. I can recall a huge sense of deflation after the meeting– it was like pummeling a blancmange, and I got no satisfaction from it.

Not that it was just the local UUP I engaged with. I appeared regularly in print in the national press and on-air and repeatedly referred to the UUP as "Vichy Unionists". I thought I was the person who had coined this acidic phrase, but Alex Kane, a strategist for the UUP and one of their brightest thinkers, beat me to it, a fact I was glad to acknowledge to Alex. He and I have remained friends over the intervening years, and people like Alex represent the best values that the UUP could stand for, had it the wit to recognise this. My sniping at the UUP seemed to annoy them and a highlight for me was when David Trimble made sarcastic reference to me in his speech at the UUP Annual Party Conference! He implied that Robert McCartney wrote my material, which greatly amused both of us. Bob wrote his material and I wrote mine and never the twain did cross.

Using my own political antennae on the ground, it was obvious that David Trimble's shameful decision to sit in power with the likes of Martin McGuinness was being received very badly by local people. On the election trail in 2001, I don't think I have ever encountered such visceral hatred towards a politician as that which I heard directed towards Mr. Trimble. Enraged people came out on several occasions to berate me – thinking I was an Ulster Unionist, a misunderstanding I was very quick to correct in the interests of my continued well-being! I can only imagine what it was like for the Trimble team, and one had to admire their tenacity and sprinting ability.

That said, he got himself re-elected - but this time with a diminished majority and with a number of nationalists and republicans tactically voting for him. But even though Trimble downplayed the anger of the unionist people and continued to posture as if he could operate without a popular mandate, the reality was that he was increasingly isolated.

Between 2003 and 2005, even the media could not stop the constant stories of fractious in-fighting that characterised the party. Trimble's Torquemada was to be found in the diminutive form of Lagan Valley MP, Jeffrey Donaldson. Jeffrey constantly badgered the Trimble position on power-sharing with terrorists and showed great principle at the time. I recall writing to him encouraging his stance and hoping that his view might prevail. The irony here was that but a few years later, Donaldson would jump ship, join the DUP, and would find himself advocating sitting in power with IRA/Sinn Fein!

I don't believe any electorate like to see a divided party – it certainly did for my old party the UKUP - and the endless public schisms and convulsions of these years would spell catastrophe for the UUP. Back in 2000 Trimble talked of the "constructive ambiguity" that lay at the heart of the Belfast Agreement/Good Friday Agreement. But that's a rather high sounding expression for a low down attitude towards the electorate. Trying to obscure the truth is a most unwise course of action as, sooner or later, people will figure out that they have been misled, and then they will take their revenge on the political party that has been caught out. For years, the mainstream media portrayed Trimble as a political colossus, who bestrode the political stage, and, even when knocked down, he would always come up smelling of roses. That bloom instantly vanished in the aftermath of the 2005 general election results.

Where the UUP had ten MP's, they were now reduced to one. This was a stunningly bad result, and, fittingly, David Trimble even lost his own seat! It was, of course, absolutely inevitable but might have been prevented with a degree of political modesty and a more collegiate approach to party management. In fairness to David Trimble, the very structure of the Ulster Unionist Party did not lead to effective management, but he had been given enough years to change that. There were, of course, more than a few within the UUP who realised that they were jumping off the cliff again, but none of them had the killer instinct to stop Trimble, and so their political fortunes perished on the rocks with him. The scale of the wipe out was so great it made international news, and even the mainstream media could no longer put a brave face on it.

On the 7th May 2005, David Trimble resigned from the position he had held since 1995 blaming Tony Blair for "*indulging Republicans.*" This was true in as far as it went, but it was not the complete story, because David Trimble himself had indulged republicans. He had become detached from the feelings of the pro-union electorate, his party had behaved as an ill-disciplined shambles and in the final analysis he had gambled away the UUP's prime position within unionism and gained nothing in exchange. As Tony Blair said at the time…

"Without him there would have been no Belfast Agreement."

But without him, the Ulster Unionist Party might still have held a dominant position within unionism.

David Trimble cut a forlorn figure towards the end with the minnows circling him, but yet none of them prepared to take a bite out of their flailing leader. Throughout his time as leader, it was Trimble's misfortune not to have any serious competitors for the position he occupied. He may have had his stern critics, like William Ross and William Thompson, but the fact is that all they could do was mutter their unhappiness without having the presence to offer a real alternative. Others, like David Burnside, seemed to blow hot and cold, sometimes in favour, often against. Jeffrey Donaldson was his main opponent, but yet time and time again he hesitated to strike, insisting that it was about policy, not personality. But the personality of the leader of a political party profoundly influences the policy it pursues.

I believe that had David Trimble been a man who listened to others and who might have even accepted their advice, he might have achieved a lot more. He had a formidable intellect which marked him out as an above average politician, but this was entirely undermined by the fact that his political judgement was so flawed. The DUP had eclipsed his party, a situation which was to deepen further following the 2007 Assembly Election results.

David Trimble was replaced as leader by Sir Reg Empey, his close ally during his years in power. Empey had also sat around the Executive table with IRA/Sinn Fein, but by this time there was no fight left in the UUP to do anything different. It was to be more of the same, and, as I quipped in one interview, Sir Reg has proven his critics wrong and achieved the seemingly impossible - by making David Trimble seem like an effective leader! The UUP has become a creature of the Belfast Agreement/Good Friday Agreement, content to share political power with the representatives of an organisation that had cruelly murdered its own members. It had become morally hollowed out from within, after almost ten years at the heart of the rotten peace process. Directionless and rudderless, there was nowhere to go, and reshuffling the deckchairs on the Titanic was a poor substitute for an effective political captaincy.

So where now for the UUP? I honestly cannot see that it has much of a future. The DUP has successfully salami-sliced it from the political right, and the Alliance Party has moved in to feed on the soft left. It is so slavishly pro-Agreement, so enthusiastic to power-share with terrorists, that it seems doomed to further diminution. To recover from its seemingly terminal decline would require it adopting a new strategic direction, it would mean new faces, intelligent tactics and above all clear differentiation from the DUP. Has it got the vision and talent?

It's only representation at Westminster is in the form of the liberal-inclined Lady Sylvia Hermon, the MP for North Down. It seems unlikely that it can win back any of the nine seats lost in 2005 without drastic change, and such change is not evident. And so it is that, the North Down seat apart, the UUP has been eradicated from the Westminster parliament, ensuring that its influence on the UK political stage is marginal. The sheer scale of this defeat is hard to convey, and yet it was always going to happen once the party took decisions that went against the will of its own electorate!

Ironically, the UUP was presented with opportunity to regain lost ground in May 2007 when the DUP blatantly stole its clothes and marched into devolved government with IRA/Sinn Fein. Sir Reg Empey could have chosen not to accept ministerial positions in this Executive and instead present his party as a credible opposition to the DUP/IRA/Sinn Fein axis. This would have allowed his party to credibly attack the decision-making of the new mutant Executive, but the lure of power was to prove irresistible, and Sir Reg himself even felt obliged to grab one of the ministerial positions on offer for himself. Whilst this may provide short-term rewards, it will prove damaging in the longer-term, since the DUP can point to the fact that Ulster Unionists have participated at every level of decision-making in the Assembly, and if things go wrong, as they will, all parties will have to carry the can.

The UUP famously ran its disastrous 2005 election campaign on the slogan *"Decent people vote Ulster Unionist"*. Not any more they don't. It has a charisma by-pass and no differentiated political perspectives. There are some sensible souls within the UUP who understand that the party will wither and slowly die on the vine unless there is dynamic change. Unless it opposes it will decompose. Yet, even as the party is fading away, all that is on offer is more of the same. I suspect that the current leadership carries a vain hope that the DUP will mess up in some unspecified and catastrophic way and that it can then use this to propel itself back into power. This won't be the case as by that time the UUP will be long vanished from the political radar, gone over the cliff one final time, and no one will really care.

THE ROAD TO NOWHERE

I have always rigorously followed Groucho Marx's advice never to belong to any club that might have me. And so it is that I can say that I have never been a member of any of Northern Ireland's "Loyal Orders" on sound grounds of Marxist principle, and also in the fashion belief that a bowler-hat would just not suit me!

That said, my father was a proud member of the Orange Order for all his adult life, and I have other family relations that belong to the Loyal Orders. I believe there are many decent people to be found within the ranks of Orangeism, and they have suffered a particularly bad press from a media entirely unsympathetic to their stated religious aims. I have never been overtly hostile to the Orange Order as an expression of loyalism to the Protestant faith and the British crown, but over the past decade I have watched this organisation suffer a defeat every bit as ignoble and humiliating as that suffered by King James and his army at the Battle of the Boyne. The only difference is that at least King James understood when he had been beaten, but the Loyal Orders remain in a curious state of denial. How did this happen; what brought this formidable organisation to its knees?

1997 was the last year that the local Orange Order lodge, Portadown Loyal Orange Lodge 1, was allowed to parade down the public Garvaghy Road in Portadown following their annual Somme service of remembrance at Drumcree Parish Church. I know this quiet parish church quite well; you see my family used to go to worship there every Sunday when I was in my early teens. Little did I realise that, in just over twenty years later, it would become world famous as the focus point for an existential struggle between Irish republicanism and British loyalism.

It's useful to consider a potted history of this annual service and the accompanying parade so that proper context can be provided for what followed.

Portadown District Orange Order comprises of 32 separate Orange Lodges with a membership of around 1,400. It has been going to this little country church in the heart of county Armagh for services since 1807. That's two hundred years of religious observance, and, during the vast majority of that time, there have been no issues surrounding this annual activity. The church service held on the first Sunday every July is a solemn remembrance of all those men from the 36th Ulster Division who gave their lives in defence of King and Country at the Battle of the Somme in 1916. There were 5104 Ulstermen who died on the 1st July 1916 and I can think of no more appropriate form of remembrance than a church service.

There have been significant demographic changes in Portadown over the past four decades, and it is the consequences flowing from these which have led to so much conflict and change, hatred and misunderstandings. Essentially, parts of the overwhelmingly Protestant Portadown area started to change as Roman Catholic families moved in. One of these areas was a relatively new housing estate parallel to the Garvaghy Road, called Ballyoran. I know it very well as, believe it or not; I lived there at the time!

My parents relocated to Portadown in the early 1970's because of the IRA terror blitzkrieg in south Armagh. They felt it would be safer for us to get away from all the murder and mayhem that characterised that area at this time. So we moved from the little village of Bessbrook to the larger town of Portadown. And we settled into the new housing estate of Ballyoran. Now this was supposed to be a "mixed estate", with Protestants and Roman Catholics living together peacefully. That was the theory, but practice was rather different. My family, like many other Protestant families was encouraged to "get out" of Ballyoran. We moved to a different part of Portadown in 1974. This vicious ethnic cleansing was the reason why, between 1972 and 1980, the Ballyoran estate became virtually 100% nationalist, just like the adjacent Churchill Park. For some strange reason, this atrocious intolerance on the part of Portadown nationalists has not been examined by the mainstream media. It is also a sad reflection on the people of Northern Ireland that showing tolerance and respect towards each other is so very low.

Violence erupted a few years later, in 1985, when nationalist residents in the Obins Street area agitated to ensure that the outward leg of the annual parade to Drumcree Church was re-routed away from their area. Looking back on it, I think that local MP Harold McCusker showed considerable prescience when he observed that this small re-routing, accepted by the Orange Order at the time, *"was symbolic of something much bigger"*. I can recall the intense bitterness felt by the local Portadown unionist community at what they saw as the heavy handed policing that took place under the command of RUC Chief Constable, Sir John Hermon, aimed at placating the agitating nationalists in Obins Street. That too was a taster of things to come. Being loyal now meant standing idly by and having your loyalism stripped away from you, it seemed.

Step forward in time, and fireworks (literally) flew in 1995 when for the first time, on Sunday 9th July, the RUC operating under clear political direction, moved to prevent the Drumcree parade's return journey down the Garvaghy Road. This led to a very serious situation around the province, but a deal was brokered at the 11th hour (on the 11th July!) to allow a parade down the Garvaghy Road so long as the parade was silent. This parade was led by David Trimble and Ian Paisley – a huge mistake in my view, and it culminated in images of these two politicians exultantly waving their hands in the air once the parade entered the centre of Portadown. Nationalist propaganda seized on this, and turned it into them *"dancing a victory jig"* at having got the parade away. Anyone who has watched David Trimble and Ian Paisley walk would realise that the likelihood of either of them "jigging" is remote.

However, there were mistakes all round. I do not believe that the Orange Order should ever have agreed to the *"silence"* condition for the duration of the parade down the Garvaghy Road. They should have instead insisted on the playing of suitable hymns as this was, after all, supposed to be a parade about remembrance of the fallen from the Somme. Giving silence as a concession, whilst small in scale, was huge in symbolism. Allowing Paisley and Trimble to front the parade was also a misjudgement, though perhaps it indicated an underlying malaise, namely a distressing lack of competent leadership within Orange Order ranks.

In 1996, the situation deteriorated. A decision was taken on Saturday 6th July to once again re-route the return leg of the Sunday Drumcree Church parade. This was a political decision dressed up in policing rhetoric, but it led to a further convulsion of violence that spread across Northern Ireland. There was outrage in unionist circles that the police force of the United Kingdom was being blatantly used to prevent such a symbolic Orange parade. It felt as if the state had turned on some of its most loyal citizens.

A stand-off took place between the Sunday 7th and 11th. I visited the Drumcree stand-off at this stage and vividly recall the sense of outrage and hurt felt by the local Orange Order leadership. I also remember and felt the sense of righteous anger myself.

However, there was also an abysmal failure on behalf of the Orange Order to tell local loyalist paramilitaries to take a hike as they tried to inveigle their way into the rapidly deteriorating situation. This has been an ongoing disfiguration on the image of the Orange Order – frankly it tolerated that which it should have abhorred. There should have been no place for loyalist terrorists anywhere near the Drumcree impasse. Those local leaders should have made a point of telling them to go away and stay away. I would say that Portadown district saw itself as being at the heart of the Orange Order, and so it expected to see a rallying from all other Orange Lodges across Northern Ireland in support of it. This did happen, and so it was that on 11th July 1996, once again, the initial decision to re-route was abandoned and the Parade again proceeded down the Garvaghy Road.

By this time, most of the media used the terms *"the Catholic Garvaghy Road"* – so assigning religion to a stretch of road. Now I'm not sure if this was seen as the highway to heaven, but it soon acquired a reputation more akin to the road to hell. I felt then as I feel now that this is a public road and is not in the possession of any group. It must be accessible to all who seek to use it, so long as they do so peacefully and lawfully. If one accepts the contention that there are "nationalist" or "loyalist" roads, how on earth can society function? Such a definition accentuates the polarisation of the community.

Tensions remained high over the following twelve months, and so it was that July 1997 came around. The political landscape was also rapidly changing, with the government about to succeed in tempting the clueless Ulster Unionist Party into direct talks with

IRA/Sinn Fein. The heightened impasse over this church parade had now entered into its third year and the political management of the event was moving into a new mode. To give nationalists their due, they fully understood the value of political propaganda and seized upon the Drumcree stand-off to parade their own agenda through an obliging media. The Orange Order showed a lamentable understanding of the importance of public relations.

At this time, my soon to be colleague, UK Unionist Robert McCartney, suggested a possible solution that would have required magnanimity and vision, both virtues being noticeably absent from the tribes in Portadown. His idea was to have the parade declared lawful and the Orange Order then to waive its right to proceed along the Garvaghy Road. His logic was that the legality of the parade would be established beyond any reasonable doubt, and that, for the sake of giving up the parade one year, it could then take place in subsequent years. He got nowhere with the local Orange Order, who instead listened to the whispered words of local Ulster Unionists and Democratic Unionists. The problem was that the standard of advice from these political minnows was poor, self-serving and would lead nowhere. There is also a certain *"ourselves alone"* mindset about Portadown Orangemen, and they were not likely to listen to a skilled barrister from North Down when they could tune in to the wisdom of local councillors whose political skills stretched all the way from A to B.

No solution was found, but ominously Labour had swept into power in the UK general election on the 1st May of this year, and the wretched Mo Mowlam was parachuted into Northern Ireland as Secretary of State two days later. Mowlam had been the co-author of a Labour Party 1988 policy document called *"Towards a United Ireland"*, though the local media chose to see no relevance between this and her current job! The idea that such a nationalist-loving fox could be put in charge of the (unionist) chicken coop was presented as the most natural thing imaginable.

The day before the parade was scheduled, Mowlam released a statement which implied that she had not taken a final decision on whether to re-route the parade. However, the tone of her statement, together with the nature of the deployment of police and troops, led many to speculate that the parade would be banned from the Garvaghy Road. On Sunday 6 July 1997 soldiers and RUC officers moved into the area adjacent to the housing estates on the Garvaghy Road and sealed off the area. Around 300 residents who managed to make it through to the road to stage a sit-down protest were moved, some forcibly, by the RUC. The parade went down the road for the last time.

Nationalists showed their intolerance by rioting across Northern Ireland. This was then used to establish the bizarre precedent that whichever side threatened the most violence would get its way! The Chief Constable of the RUC declared that he had decided to recommend that the parade be allowed to pass down the Garvaghy Road because of the threats to Catholics from loyalist paramilitaries. These were the same loyalist paramilitaries which the government had been engaging in detailed talks. This was also happening at the same time as the British government was urging the accommodation of IRA/Sinn Fein as the basis for political progress. Even in this context, the true nature of the "peace process" was apparent; it was all about appeasing terrorists at any price.

All the time the Orange Order demonstrated that it had little strategic vision and so was very vulnerable to the malicious scheming of the IRA sympathetic British government now in power. 1998 saw the Belfast Agreement/Good Friday Agreement arrive, and it was perfectly obvious that government wanted to shower the IRA with several sweeteners in exchange for their promise to cease bombing and to stop murdering. The real permanent cessation, unlike the phony IRA cessation, was going to be that of any "Orange Feet" walking along the Garvaghy Road. To nobody's surprise, the 1998 Drumcree parade was re-routed, this time by the government appointed "Parades Commission" – a quango aimed at pretending this was a "*local decision.*"

Thousands of troops and RUC officers were deployed in preparation for the march. The British army built a large barricade on the road which links Drumcree Church with the Garvaghy Road and dug a trench, which was then lined with barbed-wire, through adjoining fields. I recall visiting the site one evening just after they had completed this work and, irony of ironies, the fields of Drumcree now more closely resembled the fields of the Somme. Mud was everywhere and the scene was cast in the glow of a blood red setting sun. British soldiers stood there prepared to do battle with those Orangemen who wished to parade in remembrance of British soldiers who perished at the Somme. IRA/Sinn Fein strategy was working out perfectly.

It's also worth pointing out that many unionists fully understood that the entire "*Parades Issue*" was a central part of IRA/Sinn Fein strategy. They recall reading about a lippy Gerry Adams boasting to a private republican conference in county Meath that his party was behind the protests on the Garvaghy Road, Portadown, the Lower Ormeau Road, Belfast, and other areas. According to the Irish State broadcaster, RTE, they had a transcript of a speech made by Adams in Athboy. The crucial part of Mr. Adams's speech reads:

> **"Ask any activist in the North (Northern Ireland)\ did Drumcree happen by accident, and they will tell you 'no' ..... three years of work on the Lower Ormeau Road, Portadown, and parts of Fermanagh and Newry, Armagh and Bellaghy, and up in Derry. Three years' work went into creating that situation, and fair play to those people who put the work in. And they are the**

**type of scene changes that we have to focus in on, and
develop, and exploit."**

Mr. Adams candid admission is rarely discussed as it does not fit
into the media narrative that it was all about KKK-style Orange
Order bigots seeking to impose themselves in Roman Catholic
areas. Yet it is clear that IRA/Sinn Fein sought to first ethnically
cleanse target areas, using the likes of a large housing estate as
a demographic Trojan horse from which it could then further
agitate.

Similarly downplayed was the fact that the primary spokesman
for these concerned Garvaghy Road residents, Brendan McKenna,
just happened to be a convicted IRA terrorist whose previous
contribution to life in Portadown was to play a part in the
1982 IRA bombing of the local Royal British Legion Club! Mr.
McKenna received concurrent sentences for a fire-arms offence,
false imprisonment and hijacking. He was one of two masked
men who held a Churchill Park family hostage for three hours
while their car was stolen. Of all the people in Portadown to be
chosen as the public spokesman for the Garvaghy Road residents,
McKenna was the most provocative imaginable. That, of course,
was the entire point since IRA/Sinn Fein strategy was to force the
Orange Order to seek permission from a convicted IRA terrorist to
hold their annual parade. All around Northern Ireland, *"concerned
resident groups"* sprang up and curiously their spokesmen just
happened to be convicted IRA terrorists, such as Sean Murray
and Gerard Rice. Naturally the media paid scant lip service to the
outrage this caused to the unionist community which the IRA had
been slaughtering for decades.

1997 was to be the last time that Portadown Orange Order was to
be allowed to travel along the Garvaghy Road. The following year
saw a grim finale to this event. The government, via the lickspittle
Parades Commission, had re-routed the return leg of the parade

one further time. Yet again, the stand-off occurred with barbed wire and army vehicles blocking the route back from the church. This was on 5th July, and pressure started to build up as the 12th July approached. It seemed that the Orange Order was determined to force its right to proceed along the Queen's highway, and I fully supported them in that right.

There were many road blocks across Northern Ireland and many foolish events. A large tree opposite my house was cut down late one evening in a minor act of gross stupidity. Tempers were high and there was a sense of impending crisis. But the government was playing for high stakes, and so the impasse reached the 12th July, the biggest event in the year for unionists. A major confrontation loomed but then something terrible and entirely unexpected happened.

At roughly 4.30 am on the morning of Sunday, 12 July 1998, three young boys (Jason, Mark and Richard Quinn, aged 8, 9 and 10 years old) were burned to death when their home was fire-bombed in an alleged sectarian attack. This was blamed on the Orange Order or at least on some of its' supporters. The effect was instant, with most people absolutely sickened at this tragic loss of young life. The Drumcree protest continued but political support for it drained away. Support from Orange Lodges outside of county Armagh wilted. The murder of these young boys killed off the fight in many of the Drumcree protestors, and the media rushed in to attribute blame on to the Orange Order, implying that it had the blood of innocents on its hands.

However, there is a fundamental problem with the conventional argument disseminated by the media that these repulsive murders were in some way carried out by "hotheads" in support of Portadown Orangemen. The local police asserted that the terror group, the UVF, had carried out the arson that led to their deaths. The UVF did not support the Portadown Orangemen. The PUP, the political propagandists for the UVF, did not support the Portadown Orangemen. It is also said that the boys' uncle had a feud with the local UVF thugs. The argument has been made that these murders were the result of this feud. Since government policy was the primary beneficiary of these murders, perhaps more probing questions should have put in that direction? Spokesmen for the Orange Order tried to argue that there was no connection between this incident and the situation at Drumcree, but the media refused to countenance it. It was trial and conviction by media.

Over the next year, support for the Orange Order faded away. I remember visiting the most senior Orangeman in the district, Harold Gracey, one tranquil afternoon at Drumcree Church where a permanent vigil was being held in support of the right to parade. Harold was in his little caravan, just beside the church. My impression of him was of a very decent man, straight-talking, not at all media savvy. He was so obviously a Portadown man, in his early '60's, and was surrounded by men of a similar age to him. Harold was a proud man, and if the rest of the Orange Order leadership had been made of the same sterling stuff, then they might have prevailed. By this time, I was clearly associated with the UK Unionist Party, and Harold expressed a desire for my party leader, MP Bob McCartney, to visit him. I think Bob thought better of it by this time. I don't think that they would have listened to him either. In politics, as in life, the moment passes.

From 2000 on, the annual Drumcree stand off continued, with the Parades Commission refusing to accept the continued requests from the Orange Order to allow it to complete its parade. Levels of media interest declined, and it became increasingly evident that this stand of principle was in fact a busted flush. Sadly, Harold Gracey passed away in 2004, and he was succeeded by a man called David Burrows who had been his deputy during the crisis years. Throughout his entire period as District Master of Portadown

District, Mr. Gracey rightly refused to accept the legitimacy of the Parades Commission. In 2005, David Burrows resigned from his position as District Master and, stunningly, accepted a role on the Parades Commission.

The betrayal of political principle was complete, and the Orange Order now had members sitting on a quango designed to prevent the Orange Order from exercising its right to civil and religious liberty. Both unionist parties were engaged in dialogue with IRA/Sinn Fein and the position of the local Orange Order was increasingly looking anachronistic.

It is ten years since "Orange Feet" last walked along the Garvaghy Road. Their ghostly echo is now just a distant memory. Former District Master, Harold Gracey, lies buried in his grave, unionist politicians are content to share power with the IRA's front-men, and the Drumcree stand-off is over in all but name. Perhaps IRA/Sinn Fein plan some final humiliation for the Orange Order – perhaps Gerry Adams and Ian Paisley will lead them down the road the next time they walk it in a cross-community display of inclusivity?

Most recently, in the run up to the 2007 Drumcree parade being banned as usual, the local Orange Order's desperation became apparent when they sought to have direct talks with the very local residents group that they spent the previous ten years refusing to talk to on principle. Now, principles were casually abandoned. Ironically, the local residents group decided that they felt no need to talk to the Orange Order! The circle was complete with Portadown Orange Order virtually begging the intolerant local residents for permission to walk down a public road.

There is most certainly no discernible leadership left to oppose the IRA/Sinn Fein created impasse. The battle of Drumcree Hill was lost by the Orange Order because it failed to understand what it was fighting against, because unionism failed to rally in support of the beleaguered Portadown Orangemen as did far too many of its own brethren elsewhere in Northern Ireland. It is clear that, as an organisation committed to upholding "civil and religious" liberties, the Orange Order has cataclysmically failed to live up to the noble ideals proclaimed. "*This we will defend*" has become "*This we will forget*." In that regard, it follows in the footsteps of political unionism.

I believe that the "*Loyal Orders*" are being reduced to becoming little more than a historical remembrance society, which will end up parading around in designated little circles, perhaps in the local Ulster-Scots Folk Park. They have become their very own sham fight. Betrayed by their own brethren, betrayed by a powerful British government intent on offering up Orange Order liberties to appease the IRA, the Orange Order lost the war although it still hasn't acknowledged this. At a time when any form of Christianity is mocked by the secular media, the Orange Order was always going to get a hard time. Had it stood for gay rights and transsexual liberty, it may perhaps have gained a better press. It is said that county Armagh was the birth place for the Orange Order. How fitting that Drumcree, located in the heart of this county, could become its burial plot.

YOU GOTTA HAVE FAITH

For many years, the Democratic Unionist Party has portrayed itself as a fearsome bulwark in the face of any attempt to coerce the pro-union people of Northern Ireland in the direction of a united Ireland. Led by Dr. Ian Paisley, the DUP appeared to offer a more working class alternative to the "Big House" unionism of the Ulster Unionist Party, even if it was the junior of the two unionist parties.

I suppose on first reflection, it does seem a little odd that I should find myself located to the political right of Dr. Ian Paisley in 2007. After all, Paisley has long been caricatured in the media as being a latter day Attila the Hun, but perhaps without the easy manners. His party has been portrayed variously over the years as political wreckers, the abominable "No-Men" of Ulster politics, red-necked sash-wearing backwoodsmen intent on retaining the Protestant hegemony. But then again, it's not just me that has been on a journey over the past decade, the DUP has also been a-changing, and how.

My first encounter with the DUP was in late 1996, and it took the form of a private meeting with its leader, Dr. Ian Paisley. At the time, as previously mentioned, I was a member of a group of local businessmen who sought to ascertain the views of the main unionist political leaders on the state of the union, and this led us to DUP headquarters, located at Dundela Avenue in East Belfast. A group of around six of us were ushered into the main conference room, and we awaited the arrival of the man that they called "The Doc." He arrived late, but made an instant impression. Larger than life, he strode onto the podium, sat down, crossed his arms, stared at us and barked; "*Well gentlemen, how can I help you?*" I immediately liked him, though found him a tad intimidating!

Like many others, I had watched Paisley's political progress over the years on the TV, and he came across as a firebrand fundamentalist preacher/politician, not averse to grabbing publicity-generating opportunities, the most famous of which took place outside Belfast City Hall in late 1985, at a massive rally to protest at the treachery of the Thatcher Government signing up to the Anglo-Irish Agreement behind unionist backs. "Never, Never, Never" he thundered to a huge crowd of outraged unionists. The "Never" to which he referred was the idea that the Irish government would have any say in Northern Ireland's internal affairs. (How things would change in later years!) The man behind this demagogic image was now sitting in front of me!

We conducted a series of questions and answers, and I found him to be forthright, honest, though perhaps a bit aggressive when his opinions were even mildly contradicted. I remember wondering at the time who in his party would argue against him and the price such people would pay in terms of career progression. Dr. Paisley's view at that time was that the British Conservative government led by John Major was not to be trusted, that the Ulster Unionist Party (or "*Official Unionist Party*" as he insisted on calling them) led by the relatively recently elected David Trimble was not be to trusted, and that he, Ian Paisley, was not going to participate in any process that would undermine the union. I awarded him top marks for re-assuring us that the union was going to be safe in his political grip, but in retrospect his reassurances entirely centred on what "he" felt was the right thing to do. The DUP may not be a one-man band, but it was pretty clear back then as to who was banging the big drum!

Only a few months after this meeting, the government behaved as delinquently as Dr. Paisley had forecast. Tony Blair was now Prime Minister, and Labour had replaced the hapless Conservatives as the party in power in May of 1997. In July, the IRA graciously agreed to a tactical cessation of mass murder, and IRA/Sinn Fein was admitted to the political talks process. Political wrangling between the Ulster Unionists, the SDLP, IRA/Sinn Fein and the governments of the UK and the Republic of Ireland culminated on the 10th April of the following year in the shape of the Belfast Agreement/Good Friday Agreement.

The DUP, along with my own Party the UKUP, refused to participate in what we concluded was a process with a predetermined outcome. There were strenuous efforts made to achieve a united unionist front in this regard, but, for reasons outlined in my analysis of the Ulster Unionist Party, this was not to be. It is a pity since the implications of a divided unionist front were to have long lasting consequences. The enduring maxim that a house divided will not stand, well understood by all unionists, was ignored, but not from want of warning. The political agreement reached was in reality a sordid deal between the IRA and the British government, with token unionist involvement required for public consumption, and it was now going to be offered to the people of Northern Ireland in the form of a Yes/No referendum.

The DUP, along with the UK Unionists, found itself in the vanguard of opposition to the provisions of this corrupt deal. We were appalled at the prospect of convicted terrorists being released from captivity, at the plan to destroy the RUC and to put terrorists into government. We were horrified at the plans to create all-Ireland bodies and to institutionalise the role of the Irish government in Northern Ireland's affairs. Everything contemplated ran against traditional unionist convictions and public decency, but the largest unionist party had just embraced it all. This meant in practical terms that a campaign had to be organised to try and persuade the pro- union electorate that they should not endorse such a political deal, as we believed it contained the essence of rolling Irish unification. For some reason, the entire pan-nationalist front celebrated the deal!

And so it was that the *"It's Right to say No"* campaign was hatched shortly after Easter 1998, and I found myself back at DUP headquarters at Dundela House. There were a number of steering group meetings held for the anti-Agreement lobby, and I was present at some of these. It must be said that the DUP was generous in providing this facility, and everyone seemed committed to the opposition of the Belfast Agreement/Good Friday Agreement at this time.

The DUP's deputy leader, Peter Robinson, was the main DUP personality present at the meetings I attended, and I found it interesting to observe him up close and personal. Where Paisley exuded a larger than life warmth, Robinson radiated a deep chill. His clipped and precise manner of speaking, his coiffeured appearance, all pointed to a man who was highly organised and not to be treated lightly. I have no doubt that Peter Robinson's strategic and organisational skills have been absolutely central to the success of the DUP; he is a most impressive political animal. Then again, some animals are best caged.

I was amused during these meetings by the tension between Robert McCartney and Peter Robinson, with the former muttering dissent as Robinson pontificated on possible forms of strategy. Holding together the alliance of those who were to oppose the Belfast

Agreement/Good Friday Agreement was not the easy prospect one might have imagined, and it taught me that unionism's capacity to fracture itself can never be underestimated, even in times of crisis.

On the 22nd May 1998 the Referendum on what was touted by the global media as "*The Good Friday Agreement*" was held, and, as an exercise in media manipulation, it would have made Goebbels proud! Even the very name of it was designed to conjure up a certain sacredness that should not be denied. Those of us in the anti-agreement lobby found our air-time severely limited as the government threw the proverbial kitchen sink at it, and the final result was depressing but, perhaps, really not that surprising. Just over 70% of those who voted supported the Belfast Agreement/Good Friday Agreement, and the media were exultant. On reflection, I view this date as the day the union was struck a fatal blow, and a sufficient bloc of unionism was moved beyond the tipping point. The rest would follow in time.

There was little time to feel despondent though because Assembly elections were called almost immediately, and I found myself as the UK Unionist candidate in Upper Bann. In this unionist cockpit of a constituency, a decision was taken for a united unionist platform to be created by those of us in the "Anti-Agreement" camp, and that basically meant me, the local DUP, and a leading light in the Orange Order camp, county Armagh Grand Master, Denis Watson, campaigning together.

This gave me an insight into how the DUP electioneered and proved an eye-opener for this innocent abroad. The DUP's main figure in Upper Bann was a Portadown-based accountant called Mervyn Carrick. There was also a husband and wife team, William and Ruth Allen. All three were members of the Free Presbyterian Church – as was I. I have to be candid and say that I found the Allens an unimpressive pair, whilst Mr. Carrick exuded the wit one

63

would expect from an accountant. That said, he was an energetic campaigner, and I lost a few pounds in weight before losing a few more pounds on my deposit!

I got the impression that the DUP would have preferred had I not been standing, and as DUP ambitions were to grow, the very prospect of anyone opposing them was viewed as near blasphemy. Back then, I was running my own embryonic business, with two young children, canvassing in the evening, and was thoroughly exhausted by the end of the campaign! I had no idea that canvassing was so tough, and I salute all politicians who pound the streets trying to obtain a vote. I think it is a good thing that politicians are forced to go out and seek a mandate from the people, but, by the same token, once voters encounter politicians, it surprises me that anyone would vote for them.

The United Unionists got two candidates elected to the Assembly – 1 DUP in the form of the charismatically-challenged Carrick and 1 for the Orange Order in the shape of Denis Watson. In the late autumn of 1998, the DUP's Peter Robinson observed…

> **The sky is not less grey because the blind man does not see it. Equally the danger of this Agreement is not less real because 71% of the people do not see it."**

The year after the Assembly election, 1999, saw some unionists trying to bring out, public opinion to save the Royal Ulster Constabulary from what we saw was its looming demise at the hands of government appointed hit-man Chris Patten. Patten had been tasked to produce a report on the future of policing in Northern Ireland and, since the IRA required the emasculation of the RUC as a key requirement of its participation in the political process, it was obvious that Patten would axe the RUC.

Along with my friend, David Hudson, I organised a local public meeting in Banbridge and spoke at others around the province. Looking back, it was obvious from the modest attendance that, whilst there was disquiet at what was looming, there was not enough will to stop the axe from falling. The people I felt most sorry for were those brave RUC men and women who carried the mental and physical scars of terrorist barbarity and who were offended by the notion that it was they that needed to be *"reformed"* – not the terrorists! The shape of peace process Ulster was slowly emerging from the peace process slime and it was hideous.

These *"Save the RUC"* meetings culminated at a *"monster rally"* held in the Ulster Hall the September of that year. I did not speak at that event, but it was very well attended and I remember meeting up with a DUP Assemblyman after the meeting. I can still recall being shocked by the sheer cynicism he displayed towards the public. He felt there was NO chance of the RUC being retained, but he said words to the effect that "David, we have to be seen to be doing something" with a smile on his face.

There were also changes within the local DUP, and I became friendly with David Simpson – the future DUP Member of Parliament for the constituency – and I had known the amiable Stephen Moutray, a future DUP MLA, for several years previously. Both gentlemen were also Free Presbyterians. I liked them both, and there was some discussion amongst us ahead of the 2001 general election. I was asked to write an endorsement for the DUP's David Simpson election literature, and I gladly did so. In the event, he did not win, but his profile was substantially raised, and the DUP in Upper Bann morphed into a viable alternative to the ageing local Ulster Unionists. David Trimble's deep unpopularity with the local electorate helped the DUP gain local ascendancy, although the media pretended otherwise and fantasised that Trimble was still the major vote puller in this constituency. He was a vote loser, but the media had to sustain his image at all costs.

My relationship with the DUP faded after the 2001 general election. I ceased having much contact with them, and, when the Assembly election of 2003 was called and two DUP MLA's were now returned to Stormont from Upper Bann, that really was the end of days. You see, the thing about the DUP is if you're not in the tribe and worshipping at the shrine of "*The Doc*" then you are nowhere. It's almost a religious cult – though whether the structure and discipline will hold when Papa Doc is no longer around is another question. In my opinion, Dr. Paisley's son, the lobster-fishing enthusiast Ian Jnr, lacks the big personality of his father, and I have found him a cold fish on those rare media occasions when we have encountered each other. That said, I also think it is a very hard act he has to follow, and one should not be uncharitable towards him, but he does not strike me as a leader of men. His political fate seems to be linked to that of his father, and the future may not be that rosy for the Paisley dynasty once Ian Snr exits the stage.

However, the DUP manifesto position outlined in the 2003 Assembly election, and then again in 2005 at the general election, was carefully calibrated to persuade voters that the DUP had been re-born, so to speak; and whilst they opposed the position of the Ulster Unionists they were offering positive policies. That said, there was still bellicose language in their election communiqués such as…

> **"Republicans are under the cosh and a new confident and dynamic unionism possesses the high moral ground. The Unionist community does not want to go back to the bad old days when the UUP was in charge and conceded daily to Sinn Fein/IRA"**

Oddly enough the DUP policies could only really be enacted if the DUP were to enter power-sharing with IRA/Sinn Fein and so there was a seeming contradiction at the heart of DUP thinking.

The manicured language was all about offering *"Leadership to put things right"* – and the DUP provided a coherent energetic and, above all, united alternative to the divided fractious and tired Ulster Unionist Party. Quite how things were to be put right was left rather vague, and the tone was directional, not specific.

The DUP has longed to become the largest Unionist Party, and, following its massive electoral success in 2005, reinforced again in 2007, this is now demonstrably the case. It has effectively replaced the clapped out rudderless Ulster Unionist Party, and may almost completely annihilate that party over the next five to ten years. The DUP has 9 out of the 10 unionist MP's at Westminster; it has 3 members in the House of Lords – including Dr. Paisley's wife Eileen; it has 36 MLA's at Stormont; it has 183 local councillors – the DUP has undeniably become the torch-bearer for unionism. And that's the problem. You see, I do not believe that the DUP puts the long term survival of the union top of its list of priorities. The DUP puts the survival of the DUP top of its list of priorities, and the realisation of political power is the driving force within that party.

Some see IRA/Sinn Fein and its united Ireland intentions as the greatest threat to the survival of the union, but I consider the DUP as constituting a bigger and potentially more lethal danger to the Union. Why? Because it is little more than a unionist version of Sinn Fein, it is little Ulster nationalism incarnate, and nowadays it lacks any opposition to temper its worst excesses. It has swept away the Ulster Unionists, and has no effective political opposition to its ambitions. With devolution as its holy grail, the DUP has always been susceptible to pursuing a path which leads away from the union. The DUP will decide what it will do and thinks it is now clever enough to sell this to the unionist electorate, and, since it puts power first, it could potentially accept an amelioration of the union as a price worth paying so long as its grip on power is enhanced.

One of the biggest challenges for the DUP was how to triangulate within unionism so that it could accept all the major provisions of the Belfast Agreement/Good Friday Agreement whilst simultaneously giving the appearance of resisting them. That is where the so-called St. Andrew's negotiations of autumn 2006 came into play. In essence, the UK and Irish governments provided the political backdrop for this deal, after extensive talks with the DUP and IRA/Sinn Fein. All the other Northern Ireland parties were resigned to being bit part players. The idea was to provide cover for the DUP so that it could claim that it had "re-negotiated" the Belfast Agreement/Good Friday Agreement and achieved a mighty victory for unionism. At the time, Paisley boasted that…

"Unionists can have confidence that its interests are being advanced and democracy is finally winning the day. Delivering on the pivotal issue of policing and the rule of law starts now."

But the reality of the situation was that the DUP had done nothing of the sort. It had merely connived with the British and Irish governments to accept a series of meaningless linguistic evasions and pretend that these were substantive political concessions. The Belfast Agreement/Good Friday Agreement, rejected in whole by the DUP, remained intact, but its dreary exterior had been given a fresh new lick of paint in time for the coming elections.

At the beginning of 2007, some unionists worried that the DUP would try and find some way to share power with IRA/ Fein. Few conceived the degree to which this would happen. Indeed in anticipation of this, DUP spokesmen decided to stop referring to the republican movement as Sinn Fein/IRA. The IRA got at least decommissioned from the public utterances of its representatives! The reasons for this were to become clear shortly after the March 7th elections. Speaking back in 2006, DUP leader Ian Paisley could NOT have been more explicit. He said that it would be "*over his dead body*" if IRA/Sinn Fein got into power. His deputy, Peter Robinson declared that,

"It could well take a generation before the republican movement divests itself of the criminality endemic within it".

Such brave and reassuring words, designed to sooth the beating breast, but all completely worthless. The DUP entered the election posturing that they could be trusted to get the best deal for unionists. They were careful to suggest that there was little chance of them doing any deal with the IRA, and they referenced to their history over previous years before rejecting any such prospect.

Meanwhile, they faced an Ulster Unionist Party that was in favour of power-sharing with IRA/Sinn Fein. There were a small number of independent unionists standing on a *"No terrorists in government"* manifesto, but none of these, including Robert McCartney, carried the necessary clout of a Party organisation behind them. The DUP emerged victorious, carrying the overwhelming support of those unionists who could be bothered to vote. It seemed that those unionist voters who were concerned about DUP intentions decided at the last moment to put their faith in Dr. Paisley. Within two weeks of the election, the DUP and IRA/Sinn Fein were preparing to share power in a restored Assembly.

The speed with which the DUP moved shocked even the media, who were delighted to see Ian Paisley and Gerry Adams sitting side by side. The impact on the general unionist electorate was considerable, but the DUP had waited until the votes were secured before revealing their embrace of the IRA's propagandists in Sinn Fein. The brutal reality is that there was nothing that could be done about it. Of course, not all members of the DUP were prepared to go along with the Damascene conversion to power-sharing with terrorists, and the DUP's sole MEP, Jim Allister, resigned from the party in sadness thoughtfully noting that…

Sinn Fein, in my view, is not fit for government. Nor can it be in a few weeks. I have fought a protracted battle within the party over recent months against a premature DUP/Sinn Fein government. I now have to accept that this battle is lost."

There were also a number of resignations from DUP Councillors, most notably in the Paisley heartland of Ballymena. Again, these were discounted by a media which had fallen in love with the man it once loathed. Now that Paisley was fully on-board with the "peace process", the media dutifully dismissed all these resignations as just a little local difficulty, implying that those who had resigned, having served the Party for decades, were just cranks. Predictably, all those DUP MLA's elected to the Assembly stayed loyal to their party, and time was to prove that none of them would dissent from the looming partnership with the IRA's proxies. In that regard alone, they were to prove even more gutless than their Ulster Unionist counterparts.

On May 8th, history was made when Dr. Paisley became First Minister of the Northern Ireland Assembly with Martin McGuinness, the self confessed former IRA commander, as Deputy First Minister. The event was televised around the world and the MSM rejoiced at this "*miracle.*" Speaking to the assembled masses of the international media Paisley said,

"I believe that Northern Ireland has come to a time of peace, a time when hate will no longer rule. How good it will be to be part of a wonderful healing in our Province"

As he said this, the IRA Army Council remained intact, IRA decommissioning remained invisible to all but two "independent witnesses", the IRA refused to disband and republicans remained committed to the destruction of Northern Ireland as a part of the United Kingdom. In the autumn of 2007, the family of 21 year old Paul Quinn alleged their son had been bludgeoned to death by local IRA men but the "*wonderful healing*" continued for some. Post 9/11, the IRA's capacity to bomb had been effectively removed. But in a clever move, it had exchanged its worthless terror inventory for a substantial position in government. Little wonder that Martin McGuinness grinned from ear to ear.

Things could only get better. There is talk of not just one, but two movies being made about the now remarkable Dr. Paisley. The media did everything possible to portray the DUP leader as a true statesman, and images of the ever grinning Paisley and McGuinness, the proverbial "*Chuckle Brothers*", dominated the media. No one ever stopped to wonder what lay behind the grins. With his political enemies in the Ulster Unionist Party reduced to bit part players, the DUP leader seemed beyond criticism. There has been much speculation about the positive relationship that the DUP leader now enjoys with self confessed IRA commander Martin McGuinness. The image being presented is that of a team, the DUP/IRA/Sinn Fein axis, united in the business of exercising executive power.

During a jamboree to Washington in June 2007, Peter Robinson stood shoulder to shoulder with the man who he had previously described under parliamentary privilege as "*a member of the IRA Army Council*"- an organisation that sanctioned the murder of thousands - and he commented how cordial their relationship had become, more smiles all round and evidence that the DUP had now morphed into a monster that embraced the IRA's apologists.

During July of 2007, there was the remarkable statement by Dr. Paisley that *"the war was over"*. What was staggering about this was the fact that the DUP, to the best of my knowledge, had not been at war with anyone. So was Paisley now turning into a spokesman for IRA/Sinn Fein, which had most definitely been involved in a killing campaign? Have we reached the point where the perfect political partnership lies between those who claim to support the union and those openly committed to its destruction, and if so, in what way can this work for the betterment of all of the people? The DUP does not enjoy criticism. It has endeavoured to move itself to the point where those to the left of it are branded "Lundy's", the term for traitors to the unionist cause, and those to the right of it are dismissed as "mavericks" and without any electoral mandate. However to paraphrase DUP deputy leader Peter Robinson...

"The sky is not less grey because the blind man does not see it. Equally the danger of the DUP to the Union is not less real because 30.1% of the people vote for it."

FOR GOD OR ULSTER?

Winston Churchill may have spoken of the "*dreary steeples of Fermanagh and Tyrone*", but Tony Blair was quick to appreciate that the many heavenly pointing spires across Northern Ireland could be used to devilish political advantage. One of the principles of judo is to use the strength of your opponent to help defeat them, and the architects of the Belfast Agreement/Good Friday Agreement were quick to appreciate that Northern Ireland's large church-going, god-fearing community represented fertile ground for propagandising on behalf of their godless and evil agreement.

It needs to be appreciated that people in Northern Ireland are much more frequent attenders at church than those elsewhere in the UK. More than 50 per cent in Northern Ireland claim to be churchgoers compared with a mere 15 per cent elsewhere. Furthermore, women in Northern Ireland are even more frequent churchgoers than men, with 61 per cent of women attending church frequently, compared with just 39 per cent men. This was a most helpful route should you wish to influence the voting intentions of a large section of the community in a forthcoming political referendum while they quietly sat reflecting in the pews of their local place of worship.

This propensity to attend church has always been a significant feature of life in Northern Ireland, and, whilst the province has not been exactly insulated over more recent years to the sad decline of Christianity, the reality remains that each Sunday morning sees a substantial turn out of people going to their place of worship. Church still plays a key role in the lives of many people, spiritually, socially and best of all from the manipulators point of view – politically.

Theoretically, these people attend to worship God, but of course there is the wonderful opportunity for the central church bodies to ensure that the believers in the pews are exposed to more earthly messages as they seek heavenly instruction. The key statistic is that almost 1.5 million people claim to belong to the various Christian churches in Northern Ireland, and, regardless of how many of these actually attend their church of preference, it is still a massive demographic that held huge political attraction. After all, if Northern Ireland's churches were to advocate the acceptance of the Belfast Agreement, aka the Good Friday Agreement, who could then stand against it on moral grounds? And if the "Good Friday Agreement" could carry the spiritual imprimatur of all the various church leaders, wouldn't that help convey a sense of almost sacred requirement to vote in favour of such a political proposition? Heaven forbid that such calculated machinations were in the minds of those pushing this political dispensation!

The nationalist community in Northern Ireland is overwhelmingly Roman Catholic in religious outlook, and, with around 680,000 people claiming to belong to this denomination, it has the singular advantage of being a united theological body. The unionist community is of course largely, though not entirely, Protestant in its faith outlook, and has around 700,000 members. However, unlike the homogenous Roman Catholic faith, it is divided into several competing churches, including the Church of Ireland, the Presbyterian Church, the Methodist Church, the Baptists, the

Brethren, the Congregationalists, the Unitarians, and last though by no means least, the Free Presbyterian Church.

However, despite the apparent diversity, numerically the Church of Ireland and the Presbyterian Church have the overwhelmingly balance of this number, with around 600,000 between them. The fundamental question to consider is how could the main Christian churches in Northern Ireland bring themselves to first embrace, and then help sell, a political deal which turned justice on its head and which clearly rewarded those evil people who had terrorised and killed members of their own congregations – even, in some cases, their own ministers?

Many church congregations had paid solemn witness to the barbarity of terrorism, and no denomination was immune to the many acts of violence perpetrated on the communities they represented. The graveyards across Northern Ireland are replete with thousands of headstones in loving memory of those butchered by the various terror gangs. Is it possible that decades of having to bury those killed by the terrorist groups had worn down the expected moral resistance of the churches? Had the churches been slowly morphing into little whitened sepulchers, all pious front but no content? Either way, they were about to play a central role in ensuring that convicts strolled free from captivity, and that the men of violence gained a historic victory over those they had terrorised.

Week in, weak out, the churches had been changing, slowly evolving into tamed creatures of the political establishment. There had also been a sustained effort from the ecumenical movement to "bring together" the large church groups, and this was seen as a good thing in an allegedly "divided community", but I do not believe this to have been the case. In moral terms, surely the only division was between those who advocated terrorism as a means of advancing a political cause and those who opposed it? A degree in divinity is not required to hold the simple view that it is wrong to kill, to maim, to terrorise. Yet the churches in Northern Ireland struggled from the very beginning in standing behind this simple perspective.

For example, the Methodist Church had been seeking to talk to the terrorists from the start of their killing campaign, under the deluded notion that dialogue with them would somehow convince them that what they were doing was wrong, counterproductive to their expressed political aims. Those in the Methodist Church who took part in this dialogue with the terror warlords undoubtedly felt that they were trying to do right, but of course the road to hell is paved with such good intentions. At no time did the IRA choose to end its killing spree after a little theological encounter. Rather than condemn and isolate the killers, it demonstrated even as early as 1970, there were some in the mainstream churches who sought to reach out and try to understand them.

The true face of terrorism was displayed on Sunday, 20th November 1983. On this day IRA terrorists calling themselves the South Armagh Republican Action Force entered the Mountain Lodge Pentecostal Church outside the tiny village of Darkley and murdered those who were attending Sunday worship in their church. The church was filled with men, women and children who at this time every Sunday evening came together to pray and give thanksgiving to God. As the congregation broke into singing the first hymn, two gunmen opened fire on the congregation killing three elders at the doorway who were warmly welcoming people to the service. The killers calmly stepped over the bloodstained helpless bodies already cut down and began firing at the congregation of mainly defenceless women and children. Fathers dived over their young children, and one man covered a 7 month old baby, such was the indiscriminate nature of the attack. Children were screaming hysterically, calling for their mothers and fathers who were lying among the upturned pews, prayer books and Bibles. All begged and pleaded for mercy as the gunmen stepped through the bodies and made their way outside. Such was their murderous intent they took time to reload their guns and sprayed the exterior of the wooden hall before disappearing into the rural landscape. The reality of terrorism is frequently painted over by those who seek to engage in conflict resolution with such monsters, so it is instructive to reflect on what was actually done in the name of Irish republicanism.

The hopelessly wooly-minded, morally-bankrupt dogma that talking to terrorists might encourage them to stop killing and maiming was destined to become the gospel for all the main churches in the following years. As well as in Northern Ireland, we would also later witness church leaders demanding that the US/UK should not seek a military solution to dealing with Al Qu'eda; these were the same sort of pussycats in dog collars, unable to conceive that there is such a thing as a "Just War." For them, Christianity equates to pacifism.

Growing up as a child during the 1960's, I have happy memories of attending church each Sunday in Bessbrook. The tone struck in that little village Church of Ireland was typically moderate and middle of the road, and whilst the Gospel of Jesus Christ was proclaimed each Sunday from the pulpit, it was communicated in a kindly manner. We were taught to love our neighbours, and, in my case, my neighbours were Roman Catholics with whom we got on fine. The idea that Protestants and Roman Catholics could not be good neighbours was a profound slur on all of the people of Northern Ireland, but it has been said so often that it is now presented as a fact when this was not the case for many, especially in rural areas.

However, from 1969 onwards, one of the other attendant features of those who attended church is in Northern Ireland, particularly if like me they lived in border areas, was the frequency of funerals that accompanied the IRA killing frenzy. I remember the night of January 5th 1976 vividly, when news started filtering through that there had been a terrible killing near the little village of Kingsmills. Ten defenseless men had been machine-gunned to death, their crime was to be Protestants in the wrong place and at the wrong time. My former Sunday school teacher, John Bryans, was amongst those killed that evening, and I cannot begin to convey the horror, the stunned disbelief, as we tried to come to terms with such savagery.

Johnston Chapman had to identify the bodies of his two nephews who also died in this attack. He said...

> **"They were just lying there like dogs, blood everywhere. If the people who did this saw them like that, surely to God if they had any conscience they would say "well we're about to cut this out."**

But there was to be no cutting out of this kind of bloodlust, and the churches continued to bury the victims of IRA, UVF and UDA murder.

In 1998, speaking of the Belfast Agreement/Good Friday Agreement, the Most Reverend Dr. Robert Eames, Church of Ireland Archbishop of Armagh and Primate of All Ireland, declared that Northern Ireland now had an opportunity which everyone should embrace wholeheartedly. He added..

> **"Easter after Easter we have prayed for peace. Easter after Easter we have said to God in our prayers give us and bring us to peace. The developments of the past few days have not only mesmerised us, not only taken our breath away, but they have in a sense said something of great importance to us as we thank God for Easter morning."**

Just so we are all clear on this, Dr. Eames appeared to have been suggesting that cutting a political deal with the IRA (aka The Belfast Agreement/Good Friday Agreement) was akin to the greatest event in the history of Christianity. He added that his message was for people to "go forward in courage" and "*to realise that we are all made in the image of God.*" He finished by telling his congregation that…

"We deserve peace. We have to grasp peace."

Even peace at any price?

Dr. Eames was not alone when it came to blatant cheer-leading for this abhorrent political deal. The Most Rev. Sean Brady, the Roman Catholic Archbishop of Armagh and Primate of All Ireland, called on people to consider the proposals carefully. "*We'll be asking people to see the positive,*" he said. I think that was a "Yes" to the deal from the leader of the Roman Catholic Church.

Joining in the appeasers party was the Most Rev. and Rt. Hon. George Carey, Archbishop of Canterbury, who observed that…..

"A truly healthy society needs to be open to change and transformation whilst always being firmly rooted in the past, and able to drink deeply from those wellsprings of truth embedded in its traditions."

One of the most firmly embedded truths in the Christian faith is that it is wrong to reward unrepentant murderers and to set aside justice to the benefit of the lawless. Not to be outdone in this co-ordinated support by religious leaders for the political process, the Presbyterian Church also came out to welcome what was on offer. It said that…

> *Recognising that many look to the church for 'moral and spiritual guidance' the Church and Government Committee has, out of pastoral concern issued its response. The response recognises that 'it is the responsibility of elected politicians to negotiate a political accommodation,' and so' the General Assembly in June 1997 encouraged politicians to enter the talks process.' The accommodation reached 'does not represent defeat or assimilation but is rather a political accommodation which could be a way out of the darkness of the last 30 years into a better future.'*

And so it went on, ad nauseum, with all the established Churches showing their lack of Christian credentials by endorsing a deal that sprung mass murderers free from prison and rewarded the barbarians that had spent the previous three decades feverishly butchering at will amongst their various congregations.

However, there was one church which categorically condemned the Belfast Agreement/Good Friday Agreement, and that was the Free Presbyterian Church, whose moderator was Dr. Ian Paisley. The FPC preached against the evil of the agreement and presented a united front in its absolute rejection of what was on offer. I can recall the passion with which Free Presbyterian Minister's preached against the ungodly deal, yet, ironically, their own Moderator, Dr. Paisley, would later sit in power with the IRA's political proxies. This would lead to Paisley being forced to step down from his position as Moderator in August 2007 in a rare moment of effective theological judgement.

It is no surprise that church leaders were enlisted by the government to sell their toxic deal. Northern Ireland Office spin-doctor, Tom Kelly, had spelt the strategy out in a leaked memo dated 4th March 1998. Talking of the need to create "Champions" for the government policy he said...

"Each focus group should be representative of a section of the wider community. Those wider groups in turn each have someone they look up to as a representative figure. We should, where possible, be enlisting the help of those people to champion our cause, e.g., Robin Eames and other churches leaders, the heads of community organisations and trade unions, and other members of the G7. While any overt manipulation could be counterproductive, a carefully co-ordinated timetable of statements from these people will be helpful in giving our message credibility with those they represent. It has the added benefit of providing a fresh face for that message, and ensuring that it is not only government which is seen to be selling the process."

The manipulation of church leaders was all too evident, and, like well-trained performing poodles, they all fulfilled the role demanded of them. But is it the role of church leaders to do the bidding of government, or is it to teach the Christian gospel? What happens if there is a clear conflict between these? And what is to be made of the fact that so many of them rallied to their political masters' bidding whilst in flagrant denial of their heavenly Master?

Another insight into the curious logic of the theological elite is manifest in the comments of former Presbyterian Moderator, Ken Newell, who claimed that…

"As you know, at the time of the Good Friday agreement, I think it was something like 45% of Protestants did not feel comfortable with it, because usually where there's change, like in Rhodesia, South Africa, Namibia or other countries where people move into a more balanced community, the dominant groups always fear losing their influence and power, and there's an element of that, a reluctance to change. But the Protestant community

> *have also had to face major changes, major changes with the police, which has protected them for 30 years of violence. Now that was difficult. Releasing prisoners through the Good Friday agreement was really, really hard to swallow, because many of these people were to return to towns and villages where they're walking past the families that they have devastated. And therefore that was hard to swallow. But both sides have had to swallow."*

This is such an absurd view that it needs carefully deconstructed, since it is also the view of much of the liberal theological establishment. For a start, comparing an open and free democracy such as Northern Ireland to the likes of apartheid driven African nations like South Africa or Namibia is a repulsive idea. Furthermore, the Royal Ulster Constabulary protected all the people of Northern Ireland and lost hundreds of officers in the process. Mr. Newell makes much of the need *"to swallow"* moral obscenities such as the release of murderers back into the communities that they inflicted so much anguish upon. But why is this necessary? Which of the Ten Commandments are negotiable? Which parts of the Christian gospel can be set aside in order to reach better understandings with those who oppose it?

In 2002, the IRA decided to offer one of its conditional *"apologies."* This time round it chose the lead up to 30th anniversary of Bloody Friday, when a blitzkrieg of 20 IRA bombs detonated in Belfast killing nine people and injuring a hundred. It offered its' sincere apologies and condolences to the families of those *"noncombatants"* that it had slaughtered. Clearly, even all these years into the *"peace process"*, the IRA had nothing to say about all those British Army, RUC and UDR personnel it had killed. It had nothing to say about the murder of all those who had provided services to the forces of law and order. A more pathetic apology would be hard to conceive, and yet the church leaders rushed to lap it up. Bang on cue, the Church of Ireland Primate, Robin Eames, said he believed the statement was a…

> **"…positive step in terms of IRA thinking. Every step no matter how faltering or restricted towards a recognition of the evils and hurt of the past must be welcomed."**

Oddly there was no mention of justice being meted out to those who had perpetrated *"the evils and hurt of the past"*, nor for that matter who were still carrying out such "evils and hurt." Even Ulster Unionist leader David Trimble had the common sense to see that it was significant that the IRA apology said nothing at all about the recent violence that the IRA has been involved in and nothing about what their future conduct was going to be." Ian Paisley Jnr. of the Democratic Unionist Party said the IRA's words were *"crocodile tears."*

But the leader of the Church of Ireland, along with his counterpart in the Methodist, Presbyterian and Roman Catholic churches was quick to welcome the words of the IRA. At every opportunity throughout the years of the peace process, the church leaders could always be counted upon to release positive press statements welcoming whatever action IRA/Sinn Fein was prepared to take. These "champions" for government policy seemed to have taken on a quasi-political role but yet were rarely challenged by a simpering media.

But not everyone in the pews shared the same enthusiasm for moral bankruptcy as some of those in the pulpits; and it is interesting to note that the number of Presbyterians attending church dropped from just under 50 per cent in 1989 to 40 per cent by 2004;, and there was a similar fall in attendance for the Church of Ireland, from slightly under 40 per cent in 1989 to 35 per cent in 2004. Perhaps it is safer for one's religious well-being not to attend those places which preach the gospel of appeasement.

The disgraceful appeasement policy endorsed by the main church leaders in Northern Ireland carries an echo from history. Neville Chamberlain's blatant appeasement of Hitler did not go without the approval of leading figures in the Church of England. The then Archbishop of Canterbury, Cosmo Lang, was an ardent supporter of the betrayal of Czechoslovakia. After the signing of the infamous Munich Agreement, Lang gave a sermon in Westminster Abbey which portrayed Chamberlain as a veritable national saviour. So there has been a long and dishonorable tradition of UK clerics using their very public platforms to back appeasing evil.

The use of religious leaders was to surface again in 2005, when the IRA selected two such men, Roman Catholic priest Father Alec Reid and former Methodist president Rev. Harold Good to provide what was termed *"independent witness"* to its alleged acts of decommissioning. Father Reid is a member of the Redemptorist order based at the Clonard Monastery in West Belfast and has long been a friend and trusted confidant of IRA/Sinn Fein leader Gerry Adams. Father Reid had further provided evidence of his alleged impartiality by claiming...

"The reality is that the nationalist community in Northern Ireland were treated almost like animals by the unionist community. They were not treated like human beings. They were treated like the Nazis treated the Jews."

He later apologised for this statement, but the damage was done - with unionist opinion outraged.

Harold Good had distinguished himself in the late 1970's by engaging in private talks with Irish republicans, and he worked with the families of convicted republican and loyalist terrorist convicts. He is credited with playing a key role in bringing IRA/Sinn Fein to the negotiating table, or, to put it another way, in

84

facilitating the IRA/Sinn Fein agenda. Once more, how could anyone possibly doubt his independence and goodwill?

Rev. Good may have declared that the IRA had decommissioned all its weapons but added that he would take all details of this event to his grave rather than share this with the public. He offered no guarantee that the arms he saw decommissioned represented the total armoury of the IRA. He offered no guarantee that all units of the IRA had participated in the alleged decommissioning process. He offered no guarantee that fresh arms had not been brought into the country before or since the alleged decommissioning. Bound by a code of silence to the IRA, all Good could offer his fellow religionists was that he saw decommissioning of some weapons, somewhere, and at some time. Since he could not explain what specifically had been decommissioned, nor in what way it had been decommissioned, people were asked to take it as an article of faith.

2006 saw the Church of Ireland for the first time publicly hold *"talks"* with IRA/Sinn Fein. Afterwards, Lord Eames, who led the delegation of the four Northern Ireland Church of Ireland bishops to Stormont, described the meeting as "positive". Lord Eames stressed the need for what he called *" full and equal participation in the structures of democracy with support for policing"*. Speaking after the meeting, Mr. Adams said he and Archbishop Eames discussed sectarianism, which he described *"as one of the biggest blights of our society"*.

"It was a public event which, I think, sends its own very positive signal," he said. Indeed it did – it showed that the Church of Ireland hierarchy and the republican leadership were like-minded, and that sent a very positive signal from an IRA/Sinn Fein perspective. How much of a jump would it be for the church hierarchy to become persuaders for a united Ireland?

When placed in a position where they had to choose between endorsing a political deal endorsed by the government or to stand for Biblical truths such as punishing evil-doers, too many within the church sided with the earthly power. But not all of Northern Ireland's clerics have proven to be men of straw. The rector of Drumcree Parish, the Rev. John Pickering, has proven that it is possible to be true to genuine Christian principles whilst refusing to cede ground to the forces of evil parading as peace processors. For 18 years, he has been the church's rector, but during the peace process years he has faced an intense level of criticism, directed at him both locally and from within the Church of Ireland in the Irish Republic. In May 1999, Rev. Pickering and his select vestry rejected a call from his church's ruling General Synod to prevent members of the Orange Order from attending morning service at the annual Drumcree parade. Such independence of spirit and conviction is admirable and a beacon of light for others within the church.

Another godly man is the Reverend Tom Taylor, a Portadown cleric who has long understood the importance of standing for civil and religious liberty without pandering to the incessant liberal need for compromise. And there are other ministers of religion, such as those who ensured that Ian Paisley stepped down as Moderator of the Free Presbyterian Church, who continue to recognise the importance of refusing to participate in the elevation of terrorism to the highest level of government.

The problem with the last decade is that various leaders of all the main churches have willfully allowed themselves to become "useful fools." Whilst their influence was limited, nonetheless they were still able to get their siren message out to the most devout parishioners, and this was aimed at swinging the unionist vote. Nationalists understood that the Belfast Agreement/Good Friday Agreement represented a good deal for them and was a further milestone on the road to a united Ireland. But the doubting Thomases of unionism needed convincing to say "Yes" to something that many felt instinctively was wrong. With religious leaders standing in the pulpits providing reassurances and talking of the importance of peace at any price, perhaps it was not that big a surprise when a slim majority decided to trust their words and go along with what was proposed. A more blasphemous use of institutionalised religion is hard to contemplate.

THE DOGS ON THE STREET

A fundamental political proposition running across the past ten years in Northern Ireland has been that terrorists need to have political representation. Applying this logic, should bank-robbers have their very own political party to represent their innate need to steal other people's money? Perhaps drug-dealers, maybe even rapists, deserve a political voice to advocate their depraved value systems? If not, why then are terrorists elevated above all others?

The simple answer is that the British political establishment needed to find an acceptable cloak to cover its negotiations with the terrorist godfathers in the IRA. Whilst it might be deemed as somewhat problematical to have masked terrorists trooping in and out of the corridors of power in London, having their political proxies come in and out would be viewed as another matter entirely. And so the fiction was created that the IRA and Sinn Fein were somehow separate entities even as the government admitted that they were in fact inextricably linked together. Inextricably linked *means impossible to disentangle* but in the curious world of peace processing, just as in Alice in Wonderland, words came to mean whatever the government wanted them to mean, neither more, nor less.

Essential to the illusion of a "peace process" is the notion that everyone has something to gain from it. Of course, that is not necessarily the case, and some may have a lot to lose in the Northern Ireland peace process. The British and Irish governments, together with IRA/Sinn Fein, had the most to gain from their participation in it. The British Government sought to secure the safety of the commercial heart of the UK from devastating IRA bombs, whilst the Irish government and IRA/Sinn Fein wanted to advance their shared objective of bringing about a united Ireland. However, there was the small matter of the disgruntled "loyalist" terror gangs to be addressed. How could they be brought into the process? Weren't they opposed to Irish unity, after all? Didn't they claim to be defending Northern Ireland from those who wished to destroy it? How could such self-declared "loyalists" buy into a process aimed at subverting the wishes of the loyal British citizens of Northern Ireland?

These terror gangs operated under various names, but the Ulster Volunteer Force (UVF) and the Ulster Defence Association (UDA) were the two main groups at this time, and who delighted in carrying out some of the very worst atrocities seen in Northern Ireland. It's useful to recall just how vile these terrorist organisations actually were, and, sadly, there are so many examples of their depravity. The UVF had bombed McGurk's bar back in 1971, murdering fifteen people. It bombed Dublin and Monaghan in 1974, killing thirty three people, the single biggest loss of life during this period. The UVF is thought to have murdered at least four hundred and twenty six people and has a chronology of killing defenceless civilians. A more cowardly gang of killers would be hard to conceive.

The UDA, its' rival in murder, may have killed less people than the UVF, but had proven every bit as savage. Examples of its commitment to creating a kinder society included the Greysteele massacre in 1993, when it's thugs viciously shot to death eight innocent people at the Rising Son pub in that little county Londonderry village. In another example of the random violence that typified this organization it killed five people in Sean Graham's bookmakers on Belfast's Ormeau Road in February 1992.

By any definition, these terror groups were steeped in the blood of innocents, and their only contribution to Northern Irish society had been pain, misery and grief. Like parasites, they fed off the local community they infested, bullying and brutalising, dealing out drugs and misery. This naturally made them central to the process being planned by government. One of the fundamental differences between Ulster unionism and Irish nationalism has been the general reluctance of the pro-union union electorate to vote for parties which were clear fronts for terrorism. This has always annoyed apologists for the IRA, since their propaganda requirement is to suggest that "one side is as bad as the other." Whilst the UVF and UDA were every bit as evil as the IRA, the real difference was that there was no significant electoral support for those who acted as the mouthpieces for loyalist terrorism. That the UDA and UVF did not enjoy more popular political support amongst the pro-Union union electorate was a problem for the UK government. In itself, that truth speaks volumes as to the moral values of peace processing and is a clear indicator that the requirements of killers, of thugs, bombers and gunmen were uppermost in the minds of the political puppet masters behind all this appeasement.

The UVF was represented by the Progressive Unionist Party, and the UDA was represented by the Ulster Democratic Party. Neither of these had any obvious electoral appeal, and, indeed, the very names of these parties was testament to the neo-Orwellian speak that typifies the peace process. There was nothing that was in any way progressive or democratic about the UDA and the UVF, and the fact that their political proxies adopted such terms to describe themselves was surreal. Yet, as the political process developed during 1997 and into 1998, the PUP, and to a lesser degree the UDP, became the new darlings of the media. They suddenly blossomed as everyone's favourite neo-unionists, and their spokesmen were fawned over as exciting and authentic new voices even as they struggled to pull together two or three coherent sentences. The whiff of cordite that hung around their utterances seemed to stimulate even more media attention.

The leader of the PUP was David Ervine. He was a convicted terrorist. Ervine had been arrested in November 1974, while an active member of the outlawed UVF. He was driving a stolen car containing five pounds of commercial explosives, a detonator and fuse wire. Fortunately he was stopped before he could conclude his mission and was sent to prison for eleven years. Ervine explained his terrorist past away by claiming he had been affected by IRA atrocities he had witnessed in Belfast. The fact is that thousands of others also experienced such horrors without then trying to replicate them.

Alongside Ervine in the PUP leadership was Billy Hutchinson. Hutchinson had also been a member of the UVF and was a convicted murderer. He had killed two Roman Catholic men on the Falls Road in 1974. Both Ervine and Hutchinson came under the influence of Gusty Spence as they served their time alongside him in prison. Spence, another convicted murderer, became a political guru for Ervine and Hutchinson. It's worth pointing out that the UVF continued killing, maiming, drug dealing, extorting and indulging in every imaginable form of criminality even as the PUP was being treated as the new political aristocracy within unionism.

Not that the Ulster Democratic Party were any better. Linked to the UDA and UFF, this group was led by Gary McMichael. His father, John, had been a UDA terrorist during the 1970's and 1980's and had been murdered in a car bombing in 1987. John

McMichael had felt that the UDA needed a political wing, and hence the UDP came into being. Gary took over the political leadership of this group after the brutal death of his father. He and a man called John White became the public spokesmen for the UDP as the "peace process" gathered steam. John White was, yes, you've guessed it, another convicted murderer. White was responsible for the brutal murder of the Roman Catholic SDLP Paddy Wilson, who was hacked to death in 1973 along with Irene Andrews, Wilson's Protestant assistant, who had her breasts cut off in the attack. White confessed to the murders and was sentenced to life imprisonment.

So it was that McMichael, White, Ervine and Hutchinson became the "Fab Four" of mutant unionism, at least as far as the media was concerned. The fact that between them they could not muster any significant electoral support from ordinary unionist voters was almost a total irrelevance. They were walking, talking "unionist" doppelgangers for IRA/Sinn Fein, and this made it all the easier for them to be herded into the democratic tent.

I can recall my first encounter with Mr. Ervine during a BBC Radio Ulster current affairs programme. My party, the UKUP, did not engage in any way with those we termed the political spokesmen for terrorism, and that certainly included the PUP, so I was very careful to direct all my responses towards the host of the programme, the now deceased Barry Cowan. Ervine simmered with hostility towards my party, and I felt that the editorial line being followed by the BBC at the time was to endorse the "home-spun" wisdom of this "man of the people". To bring up the ongoing criminal behaviour of the UVF was deemed unhelpful by the media at this time, even as its own news bulletins reported on the "paramilitary style" murders and maimings being carried out by these hoods. Ervine was given the full five star media treatment, and, even as he strangled the English language with his verbosity, he was hailed as something fresh and new.

Those of us who opposed the Belfast Agreement/Good Friday Agreement had a shared understanding of not engaging in any form of dialogue with the new mutant unionists, just as we also refused to talk to IRA/Sinn Fein. This seemed the only logical and morally consistent approach. Because we refused to countenance them, the PUP and UDP were particularly hostile towards the DUP/UKUP, and I remember some PUP members breaking into a live DUP press conference and heckling Dr. Paisley. Bully boy tactics were allowed in the new politics, it just depended who was doing the bullying. I recall the media exulting at the idea that the former bully boy DUP'ers were now themselves being bullied.

My fundamental problem with these mutant unionists was that I viewed them as little more than tatty third rate copies of IRA/Sinn Fein, and that their only relevance came from the illegal guns and bombs held by those they had links to in the terror groups concerned. To allow such people to sit at the table of democracy devalued and corrupted it. It may have also been realpolitik but for moral dummies. They talked about the "insight" and "political analysis" they provided for the murderous thugs in UVF/UDA, as if this had any merit. It did not. Did they call for these terror gangs to immediately disband? Did they insist that they cease all criminality? Did they focus all their efforts on getting the UVF and UDA to go away forever? Instead, just as on the republican side, all they did was to convey a form of faux legitimacy upon the terrorists that they represented. They were not "loyal" to anything but their own sectional, pecuniary interests, and no self respecting unionist should have had any dealings with them.

However, in my experience, there has also been a tendency in some unionist circles to look upon the UDA and UVF as "our" terrorists, when in fact they were nothing of the sort. I never saw the difference between one set of butchers and another, and the majority of unionists also saw it this way, but unfortunately not all. So it was depressing but not very surprising when the Ulster

Unionist Party gleefully joined forces with the PUP and UDP in order to gain the political arrangement that led to the Belfast Agreement/Good Friday Agreement. David Trimble thus not only legitimised republican terrorists by cavorting with IRA/Sinn Fein delegates but also gave spurious credibility to their "loyalist" equivalents. Using the extra political numbers provided by the PUP/UDP delegates at the political talks, the UUP was able to feign that "the majority" of unionists favoured the corrupt deal brokered by government. The mutant unionists had thus fulfilled the function they had been created for.

In the elections that followed the Belfast Agreement/Good Friday Agreement, the PUP won 2 seats, but the UDP failed to win any. This more or less saw off Gary McMichael and John White, and the UDP gradually folded. John White eventually fled Northern Ireland as an internecine feud within the UDA exploded. As for Gary McMichael, David Trimble did not forget him, and he was nominated to the Civic Forum, a pointless talking quango set up in 2000. I met Mr. McMichael years later on a radio debate and was irritated to have him describe me as some sort of "Alf Garnet right wing type". To the interviewers' horror, I explained that I did not take lessons from those whose political pedigree came about from their inextricable link to terror gangs such as the UDA. Naturally, I was the one chastised by the interviewer. That's the way things worked in a peace process.

However, the PUP continued as a media-driven political force even though their representation at Stormont dropped by 50% when Mr. Hutchinson lost his Assembly seat in the 2003 elections. Despite being reduced to just one seat, the PUP continued to exercise political influence, and in 2006 the Ulster Unionist Party once again demonstrated its indecent flirtation with the dark side of loyalism by formally linking up with the PUP in order to boost its clout in the Assembly. Even as this link-up happened, the UVF continued to murder, to maim and engage in every type of crime, but the Ulster Unionist Party was content to use the political advantage of having a PUP about the place. To her credit, the sole Ulster Unionist MP, Lady Sylvia Hermon, expressed alarm at this indecent link-up, but she did nothing more about it beyond issuing a few statements. To its total discredit, the Ulster Unionist Party shied away from sending a clear message that it rejected all forms of terrorist-linked political parties.

In early 2007, events took an unexpected turn with the sudden death of the PUP leader, David Ervine. His death was treated as an event of national mourning, and he was afforded generous praise from all the main political parties. From US Senator George Mitchell to UK Prime Minister Tony Blair, his passing was marked with solemn statements, and his contribution to the "peace process" was stated as a matter of fact. His early death at 53 years was clearly a tragedy for his family, but this event was presented in the media as something much more than that, and those who pointed out that, for all the grandiose political eulogies paid to Mr. Ervine, the UVF remained armed and dangerous, were dismissed by the media as begrudging enemies of the peace process.

Between the emergence of the PUP in the mid-1990's and 2007, the UVF killed more than a dozen people. An example of their evil was the murder of two teenagers in county Armagh. Andrew Robb, who was 19, and 18- year-old David McIlwaine, both of whom were from Portadown, were brutally stabbed to death on 18 February 2000. Their bodies were found on the Druminure Road outside Tandragee, a few hours after they had left a disco in the town. Such details tended not to feature too heavily in a review of the PUP/UVF's peace processing years. The fact that the UVF chose not to decommission so much as one bullet, nor hand over one ounce of explosives during this ten year period was also conveniently air brushed out of history. The UVF continued to recruit new terrorists into its ranks, and even the Independent

Monitoring Committee, a quango set up by government to evaluate the progress of terror gangs, described the UVF in its 7th report in 2005 as *"active, violent and ruthless."* Yet somehow this was not seen as an impediment to talking to those linked to these thugs.

In real terms, despite all the media frenzy, the UVF was as brutal and criminal an organisation in 2007, as it has had been when the PUP signed up, on its behalf, to the Mitchell Principles in 1996. Just recall what these were:

> • **To democratic and exclusively peaceful means of resolving political issues; • To the total disarmament of all paramilitary organisations;**
>
> • **To agree that such disarmament must be verifiable to the satisfaction of an independent commission;**
>
> • **To renounce for themselves, and to oppose any effort by others, to use force, or threaten to use force, to influence the course or the outcome of all-party negotiations;**
>
> • **To agree to abide by the terms of any agreement reached in all-party negotiations and to resort to democratic and exclusively peaceful methods in trying to alter any aspect of that outcome with which they may disagree; and,**
>
> • **To urge that "punishment" killings and beatings stop and to take effective steps to prevent such actions.**

The UVF retains its weapons, it has continued to kill and maim without mercy, and so, despite the pretty words of the peace processors, the influence of the PUP has been invisible.

Not that this was seen as a bad thing. The UVF were *"good"* terrorists, the PUP was presented as *"progressive"* unionists, and the death of David Ervine actually represented new possibilities. In May of 2007, having trailed it through an obliging media weeks previously, the UVF announced that it would now play *"a non-military civilianised role."* This was received with the usual unthinking enthusiasm, though it was slightly tempered by the fact that the UVF made it clear it would not decommission its illegal weapons. Instead, it promised to put these guns and other material *"beyond reach"* but would not define what that meant. That was good enough. Although the UVF had declared a ceasefire 13 years ago, it has been responsible since then for a score of killings. But when a peace process breaks out, such barbarities are consigned to the memory hole.

Billy Hutchinson, an erstwhile Progressive Unionist Party Assembly member, provided a good example of the perverse logic of the peace process when he reflected:

> **"Guns have triggers and they need to be pulled. They were pulled because people were involved in a political struggle. The guns have been put beyond reach. They are not a danger to anybody"**

The reality is that *"the guns"* concerned were pulled on innocent and often defenceless people, Protestant and Roman Catholic. Once again, the peace process allowed those who had terrorised the chance to cover their tracks *retrospectively* whilst preening as guarantors of the new found tranquility. The more surreal aspect to this is summed up in this part of the UVF statement...

> **"We reaffirm our opposition to all criminality and instruct our volunteers to cooperate fully with the lawful authorities in all possible instances. Moreover, we state unequivocally, that any volunteer engaged in**

criminality does so in direct contravention of Brigade Command."

According to the IMC report of January 2007....

Members of the organisation were in our opinion responsible for one murder (which was not sanctioned by the leadership) and for two attempted murders (of which one was sanctioned). They were also involved in shootings, assaults and threats and in sectarian incidents. Criminality remained prevalent in the organisation, including robbery, extortion, smuggling, the sale and distribution of counterfeit goods and loan sharking"

On the one hand, the media swallows the UVF statement proclaiming its *"opposition to all criminality"*, yet on the other a government body confirms widespread UVF involvement in every form of criminality. Such deceits characterises the political process that unionist politicians were embracing. The gangsters that make up the UDA have enjoyed similar kid gloves treatment. In December 2005 disturbing rumours emerged that it had asked the government for a £70 million package over five years for a scheme to train its members in skills which would equip them for a new life. Amazingly, a spokesman for Tony Blair said that:

"The discussions are at an early stage. However the line we are taking is the same as we are taking with Sinn Fein. All of this is dependent on an end to criminality and paramilitary activity. As for the programme itself, they may come to us with certain figures but no deal has been struck. We will certainly listen to what they have to say but I would stress the figure of £70 million is the figure they want."

Government was this blatant in confirming that it was perfectly happy to discuss how much UK taxpayer's money it would pour into the coffers of the gangsters from the UDA. As these talks were going on, the UDA continued to murder and maim, but such "internal housekeeping" matters were haughtily dismissed by officialdom.

In September 2006, the first tranche of money flowed from government to the UDA. Although it was a mere £135,000, it was the intent behind that was so shocking. This was naked appeasement, the bribing of a terrorist group. Just over six months later, the government announced that it would now dish out more than £1m to another project aimed at moving the UDA away from violence and crime.

The Ulster Political Research Group, the front group for the UDA, had spent the past six months drawing up a business plan to persuade the government to fund a 3-year project. It said this could help transform the UDA into a non-paramilitary group. This was unbelievable – a sovereign British government committed to the global "war on terror" happily cutting financial deals with an outlawed terrorist group, rewarding it for not being too blatant about its criminal activities. There was little media outrage at this depravity, ten years of peace processing having ensured that it was now viewed as perfectly normal for government to pay off terrorists, to reward the gangsters who preyed on the communities they infested.

Even when the ill-disciplined rabble that constituted the UDA ranks tried to feign the idea that they were committed to "transformation", in the summer of 2007 it immediately unraveled with some "Brigadiers" showing that they did whatever they wanted. The media portrayed this as a struggle between the UDA progressives – the sort who enjoyed a game of golf with the Irish President's husband – and the UDA retrogrades – the sort who enjoyed more traditional activities such as drug dealing and extortion. In fact these men were all members of an illegal organisation, and once more the public was being exposed to the perverse myth that there are good and bad terrorists.

The fact is that institutionalising all forms of terrorism has been absolutely vital to gaining the political deal sought by the UK government in Northern Ireland. The ragbag "loyalist" terror gangs needed to be bought off and elevated in importance, just like their republican counterparts, and the creation and elevation of mutant unionist parties provided the means for this objective to be achieved. The concept that rewarding lawbreakers, killers and thugs might just bring about a more depraved society was not considered worthy of debate. The most sickening aspect of all of this has been the way in which the atrocious barbarism of the UDA and UVF has been consigned to the memory hole. The psychotic slaughter of innocent people, the seething sectarianism, the profound criminality, all discreetly paved over and recast as a historical awkwardness, an anachronistic little difficulty best left in the past. This is surely wrong.

The UDA and UVF terrorists should be hunted down and brought to justice for their crimes against humanity. Rather than wasting millions of pounds of taxpayers money on appeasing them, Government should be directing the full force of the law at gaining convictions and so delivering justice to those bereaved, maimed or in any other way traumatised by them. But to do that would be to go against the essential immorality that lies at the heart of the "peace process", and so it is that the perpetrators of acts of terror are rewarded and the victims of their evil are marginalized. In the Northern Ireland peace process, the primary beneficiaries have always been those with the power to wreck it. That makes terrorists and their Armani-suited political apologists very important people. It makes their victims an inconvenient statistic.

The introduction of mutant unionists in the shape of the UDP and the PUP to the political process did not have to be accepted by democratic unionist politicians, but their toxic presence was tolerated and in time, embraced.

> *"Vice is a monster so frightful mien, As to be hated needs but to be seen; Yet too oft, familiar with her face, We first endure, then pity, then embrace." – Alexander Pope*

ONE MAN BAND

Whereas the Ulster Unionist Party and the Democratic Unionist Party slavishly chased devolution and fought with each other over as to which would be the biggest party, there were more thoughtful people within unionism who sought to provide the electorate with a party that was not sectarian, which was pluralist in outlook and which advocated integration rather than devolution. This appealed to me, and so it was that the only political group that I have ever belonged to was the famously self-exploding UK Unionist Party!

The interesting thing about the UK Unionist Party (UKUP) is that it was never really intended to be a political party. Accidents will happen and in truth the history of the party is littered with accidents. Fortunately, we had a lawyer available!

The main figure in the party was North Down resident, Robert McCartney. He was a distinguished barrister, who had long been a thorn in the side of the Ulster Unionist Party, eventually leaving it in 1987 disgusted at the refusal of the Molyneaux leadership to endorse his candidature against the North Down Independent Unionist MP, James Kilfedder. McCartney had also famously branded DUP leader Ian Paisley *"a fascist and a fifth rate Calvin"*,

-so he was an equal opportunities insulter of the great and the good. From my perspective, this was an admirable characteristic and evidence of independent political thought.

In 1995, James Kilfedder died of a heart attack, and a by-election was held on the 15th June from which Robert McCartney emerged as victor. He became the Member of Parliament for North Down at the third attempt, and I do believe that at that moment in time he was viewed by quite a few as a new pluralist-minded liberal politician who offered a real alternative to the existing stale unionist menu. I can still recall his interview on Radio Ulster the morning after his victory and wondered if he really could be the future voice for positive unionism. It was a bright moment, and the years to follow would test the reality of the McCartney promise, but at the time I was excited that we had a first rate advocate for the union at Westminster.

Just under a year later, in May 1996, the UK government called the Forum elections, and Robert McCartney was elected on a province wide vote of 25,500. He was subsequently joined by the veteran Irish politician and writer, Conor Cruise O'Brien, and Cedric Wilson in these multi-party Forum talks. In 1997, Sinn Fein/IRA called a tactical cessation of mass murder and was instantly invited into the Forum talks by a conniving government. The UKUP delegates, true to their word, withdrew from the talks, and thereafter from the Forum itself. At the time I applauded their integrity, although noted that the media took exception to this decision, and a great cooling in relationships between Bob McCartney and the local media commenced. In a sense, the new Ice Age was beginning for the North Down MP, with the media freezing out those who did not go along with "the process."

I had known Cedric Wilson, Patrick Roche, and others who were to play a dramatic role during the later self-destruction of the party through my association with them in my role as Chairman of the non-party aligned "Business & Professional People for the Union" grouping.

Cedric Wilson was an interesting character, and it has always disappointed me the way in which he was reduced to being a two dimensional "serial protestor" figure by the media. Yes, Cedric had protested over various acts of betrayal of Northern Ireland by successive British governments, and what was wrong with that? Was he to be demonized merely because he refused to acquiesce to that with which he disagreed? The fact of the matter is that Cedric was much more than this and possessed political skills that many have not fully appreciated. He had excellent organisational abilities, and these are critical to the building of any political party. He understood the impact of effective design, vital for the communication of big ideas. He got on well with people, and I believe he was very sincere in his political outlook. He also had a good sense of humour. I don't think he was a political strategist, but he was a man who could get things done, and in my view that is the key to success in any field. Cedric played a big part in helping get the UK Unionist Party off the ground, and, despite what was to follow, it would be very ungracious not to acknowledge his contribution. Cedric was a principled unionist, and at the time I was very happy to include him amongst my political friends.

Alongside Cedric was the Bangor based Patrick Roche. Patrick had a keen intellect and was rock solid in his approach to the union. With a degree in Economics and Politics, and an MA in Political Philosophy, I found Patrick to be a good colleague, and I was particularly saddened when I could not talk him out of leaving the party. Patrick was a polished debater and was one of the very few people I have even seen unsettle Tony Blair during a TV debate he took part in back in 1998.

As the pace of political events heightened, the group to which I belonged "interviewed"David Trimble - the relatively new Leader of the UUP, Dr. Paisley, leader of the DUP, and fatefully, Robert McCartney - leader of the UKUP. I was most impressed with Bob McCartney - he was earnest, obviously intelligent and spoke in a way which resonated favorably with me and several others of the group. He had formidable insight combined with an intensity that he wanted to do all he could to help preserve the union for the betterment of all of the people of Northern Ireland.

Robert McCartney had a somewhat left of centre set of values in the broader political sense and indicated that he might take the Labour whip in the event of Labour coming to power. He believed that a Labour government would be less dangerous to the union than the existing Major-led Conservative administration, and many of us went along with him in thinking this at the time. We recalled how effective Labour MP Roy Mason had been whilst Secretary of State, and Bob believed that Labour would treat Northern Ireland honourably when in power. Judge them by what they do, not by what they say, is how he explained it to us. He was wrong in his conclusion that Labour could be more trusted than the Conservatives, the reality was neither of the two main UK political parties could be relied upon in any way by the pro-union people of Northern Ireland.

Whilst I found Bob to be an impressive figure, I chose not to join up with him at this point. Along with some others, I was trying to stay non-party aligned in the naïve belief that one could support the union without being a member of a specific party. 1998 saw the government call a Referendum on the outcome of the talks between the various local political Parties - which by then had excluded the DUP and UKUP. I was then more centrally involved through my friendship with Cedric and Patrick and attended private meetings of the "No" Campaign, along with several public meetings and rallies. Looking back on it, this was a heady time and my first full-on political experience. I was fortunate to meet most of the major unionist figures during this time and was appropriately underwhelmed!

Bob McCartney was the exception, and so, after the referendum was held and the gallant "It's Right to say No" campaign failed to swing the day in May of that year, I was invited to stand as a candidate for the UKUP in the 1998 June Assembly election. In a moment of madness - to borrow a contemporary phrase - I accepted it, knowing absolutely nothing about campaigning and with little on-the-ground canvassing support in the bear-pit of unionism in Upper Bann. David Trimble was the sitting MP, so the scale of the challenge was immense. The UK Unionist position was simple. It opposed any political arrangements which rewarded terrorists; which would release killers from prison and which would destroy the RUC, therefore undermining the rule of law. The party absolutely opposed devolution on the terms available and sought to persuade the electorate that integration with the mother of Parliaments at Westminster was the best security for the union. In that respect, the UKUP stood alone, but I feel now as I felt then – its pluralist-minded outward looking unionism was indeed the most progressive form available. I was honored to stand on such a manifesto, as I felt it was decent and principled. There were no caveats, and we had no intention of compromising on our core political beliefs. But could we sell it to the electorate?

The answer was...YES! I did not succeed in winning a seat in Upper Bann, and got 1400 odd (some might say very odd!) first preference votes. I did, however, outpoll every other Ulster Unionist except Trimble. I got virtually no transfers from the other unionist parties, and it was at that point I started to understand why tribalism is such a big factor in NI politics! In my naivety, I thought that unionists would support each other, and in particular those unionists who opposed the Belfast Agreement/Good Friday Agreement would be supportive of each other. Not a bit of it. It was obvious that the DUP looked after the DUP first and foremost, and all transfers went to the Ulster Unionists. I was very disappointed at the time but look back on it now as a lucky escape for which I remain eternally indebted to the good people of Upper Bann. However, whilst I failed to win a seat, several of my colleagues succeeded! Along with Robert McCartney, Cedric Wilson got elected in Strangford, Patrick Roche in Lagan Valley, Roger Hutchinson in East Antrim, and Norman Boyd in South Antrim. I was closest to Patrick and Cedric.

But just before the UKUP gained this significant electoral success (completely ignored by the media since its views were by then taken as a modern heresy), the seeds of self destruction had already been sown. At a meeting held in Bangor, Robert McCartney had asked all prospective candidates to agree to resign their seats if he requested it in certain circumstances. I clearly recall we all verbally agreed to this, though in retrospect the reasoning for his demand was poorly communicated. No written response was asked for, and a ticking bomb commenced. Almost straightaway, or at least after the June election and the long summer period, the mood had been a-changing in the party. I had become the Communications Director and obviously was talking to everyone, including Bob. But there were now two camps – with Bob McCartney in one and the other 4 MLA's in the other.

The party's President, Conor Cruise O'Brien, had written an article for his employer, the Sunday Independent, in which he suggested that there *could* be circumstances in which unionists might prefer to be in a united Ireland than in an IRA/Sinn Fein ruled Northern Ireland. This was like a red rag to a raging bull for Patrick and Cedric, and despite my concerted efforts to achieve some sort of peace – relationships dramatically deteriorated. Naturally, all our political opponents seized on what Conor had written and used it to suggest that we were in favour of a united Ireland. This was not the case, but his words were a hostage to fortune, and the timing could not have been more disastrous.

Meanwhile, IRA/Sinn Fein indicated that it intended taking its places in the Executive without any prior IRA decommissioning and Robert McCartney believed that should this happen, all five UKUP MLA's should resign their seats. This was going to bring about an explosive situation when it became clear that the other 4 MLA's were intending to take up their seats and resignation was not part of their thinking.

A meeting was called at Stormont in McCartney's office. The atmosphere was electric as the door closed and things kicked off. Basically, Bob felt the 4 MLA's were behaving dishonorably, and he made this clear in no uncertain terms. They responded that he was wrong and was behaving like a tyrant. Harsh things were said, and it just all went off the rails, ending in total discord. I have never been in such a bad-tempered meeting. I felt that Cedric and his colleagues no longer trusted me - fearing I was in Bob's camp. In truth, I was torn between people that I had viewed as friends now acting like implacable enemies. This is one reason why politics is a profession best avoided by any sensible person - it ruins friendships. I remember Bob ruefully observing that if you want a friend in politics, get yourself a dog!

And so it was that in January 1999, the UKUP split in two, with four MLA's going off to form the Northern Ireland Unionist Party. I did not agree with their course of action, and I stayed with Bob. Losing Cedric and Patrick was a huge blow, and the credibility of the party was terminally undermined. We went through a tumultuous period at this time, including public meetings and media appearances, as we tried to explain what had happened. Looking back, it was of course far too late. The split was very public though it would take several more years to ascertain just how lethal it had been. I suppose you could conclude that it was the winter of our discontent, and it saw the noble ideals of the party crash and burn. Everyone involved would end up losing because of it. Worse than that, it damaged unionism, because, had the UKUP stayed intact, it might well have gained a pivotal political influence which could have been used positively.

None of the departing MLA's spoke to me again during the next five years. I have since met with Cedric and corresponded with Patrick, following the sad death of his wife, Liz. I have no interest in speaking to the others. I wish that things could have worked out differently, but feelings can over-ride better judgement, and long term goals get lost in the heat of the short-term emotion.

The newly-formed NIUP had its own problems and by the end of 1999 it had expelled MLA Roger Hutchinson from its' ranks. Hutchinson had accepted seats on two statutory committees, against NIUP party policy and was shown the door by the new party. Hutchinson went on to set a new Northern Ireland political record for joining and leaving parties since he had joined the UKUP, then left to join the NIUP, then left and sat as an Independent before joining the DUP in 2001! He then resigned from the DUP in 2003 and stood as an Independent and was promptly rejected by the electorate! He had been to more parties than Paris Hilton!

Despite the debacle of the early 1999 split, that year also saw the June European election. McCartney was persuaded to stand as a candidate, and he and I were closely involved in composing the party manifesto at this time. That was quite an interesting experience, and I vividly remember the late nights trying to construct several sections of this. I have to say that during this time, I found Robert McCartney an agreeable colleague who was easy to work with and who was good company. I also think that the pressures of the split and the general intensity of the political climate at this time took an understandable toll on him.

The European campaign was difficult, coming as it did six months after the very public split and the acrimony which followed it.

We did enjoy some good campaigning days, one highlight being when Nigel Farage from the UK Independence Party came over to spend a day with us. In retrospect, Robert McCartney standing for MEP at this time was a bad idea and I wish I had advised him not to stand as it would have been the more prudent course to take. That is one of my few political regrets but being caught up in the heat of the political moment and not having the ability to stay a little distanced is all too easy.

We found the media reluctant to give Robert much publicity, and in Northern Ireland the European parliament election is somehow inexorably linked with the agricultural lobby - a group I have little time for. It is also relentlessly tribal, and it is turned into a macho exercise as to who can top the poll, a strategy with legislates against the less well established candidates. The pace of the campaign was exhausting, and it was good to finally get to the election day. I recall the count taking place at the King's Hall in Belfast and the insults thrown our way by, amongst others, the DUP's William Hay. I also remember the jeering from David Ervine, the UVF's political front-man and media darling. McCartney got just over 20,000 votes, around 3% of those cast, and worst of all trailed in behind the PUP leader, David Ervine, who got 2000 votes more. It's hard to know what to say about this other than observe the harsh fact that more people preferred to vote for a convicted UVF bomber than a man who had spent his life upholding our laws in the courts. What a brave new world we now lived in thanks to the peace process!

From 1999 to 2001, the UKUP maintained a relatively high media presence, and I was elected Deputy Leader in December 1999. It was a time for trying to re-organise the shattered party into effective constituency associations, provide it with a proper constitution, and plan a party future post-McCartney who was in his '60's by this point. During these years, he and I became trusted colleagues. My wife and I were dinner guests at his beautiful home at Cultra, and I got to see another side to him – not the public side, but a more reflective persona, a man who was immensely proud of his family and who loved the written word. His wife, Maureen, was a tower of strength to him, and she was a balanced and thoughtful person with a keen political mind herself. There is always another side to the politician, and in Robert's case the private citizen was different to how many imagined him. People used to ask me what it was like to work alongside the mercurial McCartney, and I always answered that it was just fine. He was never anything but pleasant to me, and, whilst we both were passionate in our defence of the union, there was no conflict at all between us. I know that others claim to have seen a different side to him, but I can only speak from my own experience, and I found him to be very civil man.

As well as being a Member of Parliament, Robert was also an MLA, and he and I frequently met up at the Stormont Assembly. During this period, I witnessed the gross hypocrisy of certain other politicians in unionist parties who publicly claimed that they "never" spoke to Sinn Fein/IRA representatives, whilst happily chatting away to them in the Member's tea-room. I also discerned that the UKUP was seen as a nuisance by the other unionist parties, and Robert's relationships were rocky with many of these other elected politicians. He never had any contact with the Sinn Fein/IRA or PUP/UVF front men, and in that regard I followed him, refusing to sit in the same TV/Radio room as them. That used to really annoy the local media, but why should we have provided sanitisation to those we saw as the enemies of democracy?

Events were building up to the 2001 general election and the local NI council elections which coincided with them. McCartney sought to defend his Westminster seat and the UKUP also chose to put up several local candidates for Council. It was a very busy time with degrees of in-fighting that did not help the cause. It also brought home to me that to fight elections successfully you must concentrate your resources and not spread them too thin. Unionism had been polarising since 1998, and, whilst I remained friendly with the DUP locally in Upper Bann, including future MP David Simpson and future MLA Stephen Moutray, relationships elsewhere were very raw.

In the event, the UKUP vote splintered, we did not make any breakthrough, and Robert lost his Westminster seat in North Down thanks to a Faustian pact between the UUP, Woman's Coalition and the Alliance Party ensuring the uberliberal Ulster Unionist Lady Sylvia Hermon gained the constituency. I was present at the count when the result was announced, and it was a horrible moment. We were jeered by the Ulster Unionists, the Alliance and assorted other "moderates". Robert took it all with as much good grace as one could expect in such circumstances and I felt very sorry for him. I recall thinking Lady Sylvia Hermon was less than gracious in her "victory" speech. That day was a real low. It seems to be a fact of life that it is the so-called moderates who can be the most vicious in politics.

At this point I concluded the pro-Union electorate was inherently tribal, and fundamentally disinterested in what smaller unionist parties had to say. I wondered what the point was in carrying on? Some of my associates drifted away, disgusted at the mood of the electorate. These included my right-hand colleagues in Upper Bann, David Hudson and Stephen Briggs, both men of political principle who had helped motivate me through this tough time. Things were ending. The excitement and hope of 1998 had evaporated. The media treated Bob as a combination of demon and joke. I had come to view him as a principled political intellect cursed with limited man management skills, and this was the primary fault-line that led to my ultimate political fracture from him.

He and I finished our political relationship during one very heated late night phone call in the autumn of 2001. I hung up on him – completely fed up - and publicly resigned a few days later. As it happened, this coincided with the party annual conference. I doubt it did the party much good, and quite honestly I didn't care. Looking back on it, I wish I had resigned earlier. My line at the time, and which I do not regret using, was that for a man who claimed that he was not a one-man band, Bob did like to play every instrument!

Towards the end of days in the UKUP, I had become interested in how to communicate through what was the then the growing internet, and had conceived of an on-line political journal called A Tangled Web. I tried to get Bob interested in this the year before we split, but I don't think he was that keen on the concept. I subsequently threw all my energy into launching A Tangled Web and I think it ironic that it has now outlasted the UKUP.

But though I was gone, the UKUP still staggered on. I had written hundreds of press releases for it over the years, but now these instantly ceased. Media silence now prevailed apart from McCartney's occasional perceptive articles in the regional press. From the general public point of view, the party image was reduced to that of being one man who had just lost his Westminster seat and who was now merely one out of 108 MLA's. I do not doubt for one moment that he remained true to his guiding values, it's just that people were no longer paying much attention.

He stood for re-election in the 2003 Assembly election and trailed in 5th amongst the unionist candidates in North Down, a poor result. His first preference votes were now 3374, whereas back in 1998 he had obtained 8188 votes. The writing was on the wall, but I'm not sure anyone was looking. Two years later, the UKUP stood in the 2005 council elections and achieved risible results, winning a mere 734 votes in the hitherto North Down heartland. The party really was over but still it stumbled on for another two years.

It was not just the UKUP that fared badly, in fact the breakaway NIUP, led by Cedric Wilson, melted down even earlier. It performed abysmally at the local government elections in 2001, and in 2003, it put up just two candidates in the shape of Cedric Wilson and Norman Boyd who polled just over 1000 votes between them. The NIUP was vanquished as any form of political force and a price was paid for events that had taken place in 1999.

At no point between 2001 and the autumn of 2006 did McCartney and I exchange so much as one word with each other. However, in the autumn of 2006, I was invited to be a speaker at the BBC organised "Big Rates Debate" in Belfast at the Ulster Hall. McCartney was unhappy because he was not allowed to speak from the platform to a large audience on the issue, and he may have felt that I was taking his place. He sat in the front row, right in front of me, but was generous with his applause during my speech and various interventions against the government Minister, David Hanson. At the end of that evening, on my way out of the Ulster Hall, we met and shook hands. Bob turned away from me after shaking my hand though a few of his acolytes carried on talking, pointing out to me that the BBC was using me to undermine the Fair Rates campaign. I was not impressed. I wish that Bob and I had been able to talk more freely as he was a free thinker who brought colour and rare insight to the political scene.

March 2007 brought a fresh set of Assembly elections and the final curtain. Robert McCartney lost his North Down Assembly seat, suffering the indignity of gaining only 1806 votes. He had also stood in a number of additional constituencies around Northern Ireland and received a derisory vote in each of these. The lessons of the 1999 European election had never been taken to heart. It really was the end of the line for his political career and he acknowledged this in as many words. It cannot have been easy for so proud a man to suffer such outright rejection, but such is the name of the political game. At this time, I sought to make contact with Bob with a few words of sincere commiserations - his political end may have been met with glee by many in the media and his political opponents, but I felt it right to show him that despite our differences, I appreciated his virtues and his attempt to offer an alternative brand of unionism. He had his faults, but which of us doesn't? Political defeat is a bitter pill to have to swallow, but there is the old maxim that all political careers end in failure. He has since retired entirely from any public role.

I still remain proud of my association with the non-sectarian pluralism of the UK Unionist Party. We did have some exciting times, including fascinating meetings with the likes of Peter Mandelson, John Reid, General Sir John de Chastelain, Senator George Mitchell, Mo Mowlam, Sir Ronnie Flanagan and David Trimble. I retain some good memories of Robert McCartney, and for a time I think he struck a resonance with the pro-union electorate. He was the only unionist politician I have met who I believe was genuinely sincere in his quest to protect the union. For all his flaws he was feared by the establishment and his many political opponents because he was an intelligent advocate for the union.

Every political party depends on its supporters, and there were many decent people who backed the UKUP, and I can still recall meeting with them in their various constituency associations around Northern Ireland and hearing their hopes for a better, more principled, form of unionism. Whilst politics may be a cynical game, these were people of the highest integrity. Most had left the other unionist parties disgusted at the lack of political principle and were attracted to the vision that Robert McCartney offered of a broad unionism that could include Protestant and Roman Catholic and which was pluralist, outward-looking and nonsectarian. Most of the party support base was repelled by the DUP's mixture of religion and politics and was equally fed up with the Ulster Unionist contortions.

A lot of the UKUP support was concentrated in the North Down area where Bob McCartney's profile was highest, but there were fervent supporters elsewhere, including where I lived in Upper Bann. At election time they were helpful in canvassing the electorate as best as possible, and many of them were not in the first flush of youth, so their commitment was never in doubt. These people were looking for an alternative to that offered by the two main unionist parties. Had the UKUP been able to stick together as a united team and find the financial resources necessary for political growth perhaps the course of unionism could have been changed. In the final analysis the beat coming from the one man band proved just too divisive.

I(RA) FOUGHT THE LAW

Demoralising and then demonising the forces of law and order is a primary objective of a terrorist campaign. Around the world, from Baghdad to Belfast, those who seek to uphold the rule of law are targeted, maimed and murdered and then blamed for the circumstances that led to their deaths.

During the years of IRA blitzkrieg, the forces of the Royal Ulster Constabulary, the Ulster Defence Regiment and the British Army stood between the ordinary citizens of Northern Ireland and the terrorists that infested that society, and these men and women paid a terrible price in terms of lost lives and horrendous injuries, physical and mental. Watching their colleagues die, often in the most terrible circumstances imaginable, and then fearing the knock at their door in the middle of the night, these guardians of the law worked and lived under high stress conditions and yet managed to do their jobs in a professional and courteous manner. But, in a political peace process which inverts morality, it became obvious very early on that the RUC and the UDR/Royal Irish Regiment would become sacrificial lambs portrayed as the moral equivalents of the wicked terrorists who preyed on them.

So why was it that the unionist political class was prepared to sell out the RUC and betray those officers who had bravely policed the terror campaign but somehow were deemed unfit to police the peace? Why was it necessary for them to accept that the most experienced and skilled anti-terrorist police force in the world be axed? How could it be that politicians accepted that the IRA, UVF and UDA could stay, but the RUC had to go? Did this change strengthen or weaken the rule of law? The de-politicisation of policing was a stated objective of the Belfast Agreement/Good Friday Agreement, but did this happen, and how did it impact on the topography of law and order? Is Northern Ireland a more lawful place after ten years of peace processing?

The unionist community had always viewed the RUC as defending everyone from terrorist attack and in trying to maintain law and order at a time when chaos was the order of the day. For generations, the pro-union people had placed their faith in the Royal Ulster Constabulary, and the men and women that served in the force repaid this many times over. The RUC was hated by the IRA, and 277 officers lost their lives to these republican killers, and a further 9000 were injured by these terrorists. The IRA delighted in slaughtering RUC officers, whether they were on or off duty, and this had a traumatic effect on the communities from which these officers hailed.

I vividly remember the morning of 2nd April 1981, when Constable Kenneth Acheson was brutally murdered by the IRA near the village of Bessbrook. He was fatally wounded by a booby trap car bomb. His younger brother, Noel, was my friend, and I cannot begin to express how shocked and horrified I felt at his tragic loss. His parents had to bury their son at the tender age of 23 years. What can you say about such sheer evil, the inhumanity of those who would plan and perpetrate such an atrocity on a fellow human being?

Another example of the sheer depravity of the terrorists occurred in Londonderry on the 28th March 1982, when RUC Inspector Norman Duddy was leaving Sunday church service in the Strand Road. He walked over to the car with his two young sons and was shot dead sitting in the driving seat, in front of them, by IRA terrorists. Can you imagine the horror of that moment? Can you imagine the impact on the family circle for years to come?

The decades are littered with similar vile acts of terrorism, and hundreds of families of police officers had to come to terms with the sudden and brutal loss of a loved one. At the time, there were the formulaic expressions of sorrow by the establishment, with unionist politicians declaring that the killers would not prevail and that they must be tracked down and brought to justice. In the overwhelming number of cases, however, the killers got away. Worse still, those relatively few terrorists who did get caught – such as convicted IRA bomber Gerry Kelly and convicted UVF bomber David Ervine – would later be hailed as the bright new face of politics in Northern Ireland. Those who had been actively involved in terrorism were elevated in society, whilst their victims lay in their graves. This is the shocking reality of the Belfast Agreement/Good Friday Agreement.

The RUC had the advantage of good local intelligence on the various terrorist groups, and, over the years, numerous atrocities were averted by quick-thinking and well-informed policing. Naturally, those RUC officers that served through this period became very experienced and learned the hard way how terrorism could best be countered. RUC Special Branch, in particular, was loathed by terrorists since it specialised in combating the IRA by penetrating deep into the terrorist network.

This formidable expertise was feared by the IRA, and, as the 1980's rolled into the 1990's, and the republican strategy became more nuanced, it was clear that the destruction of the RUC would be an essential price if progress was going to be made. Now, from a terrorist perspective, it made perfect sense to seek the destruction of the one police force which had made their lives such a misery. But how would the British government get unionists to acquiesce, if not accept this?

As early as early 1997, I can recall Robert McCartney and others warning that embracing the Belfast Agreement/Good Friday Agreement would inevitably lead to the destruction of the RUC. Such voices were marginalised at the time, and their claims dismissed as alarmist. In its referendum leaflet of May 1998 entitled *"The RUC has been Saved"*, the Ulster Unionists claimed:

> **"Thanks to the UUP the section of the agreement was rewritten with recognition now given to the RUC with authority delegated as the Chief Constable should decide within a unitary structure. The RUC's position has not been negotiated in the Talks and the Commission in the Agreement looks towards the adjustments which would naturally arise if terrorism ends."**

In fact, the RUC was far from safe and was facing its demise, but, surprisingly, it would be a well known Conservative figure that would plunge the knife into the Force. Conservative grandee Chris Patten was the political hit-man picked by the Labour government to chair the risibly entitled "Independent Commission on Policing in Northern Ireland." Anyone who believed that this commission did not have a predetermined agenda was a fool, but Patten was very careful to be seen to go through the usual charade of holding public meetings so he could more fully understand what the people wanted -then his commission would do what it always had intended to do anyway!

I attended several of these public consultations, and all unionists who spoke up made it clear that they did not see any need for the

RUC to be axed. They would have done better to stay at home and deny Patten and his associates the pretence that it was in any way listening to the voice of the unionist people.

On cue, Patten's commission recommended that the name, badge and oath of the 13,000-strong RUC be dropped. Union flags would no longer fly from police stations, and all portraits of the Queen would be removed from reception areas. The force was to be renamed the Police Service of Northern Ireland. New recruits would no longer have to swear allegiance to the Queen, but instead would swear an oath to upholding "human rights." In essence, the force was to be stripped of every outward and visible symbol that made it British as a calculated appeasement of Irish republican insurrectionists.

Just consider the words of the RUC oath that Patten deemed so unacceptable.

"I (name) swear by Almighty God that I will well and truly serve our Sovereign Lady the Queen in the office of (rank) without favour or affection, malice or ill-will; that I will to the best of my power cause the peace to be kept and preserved and that I will prevent to the best of my power all offences against the same; and that, while I shall continue to hold said office, I will faithfully, according to law, to the best of my skill and knowledge, discharge all the duties of the said office and all such duties as may be attached to such office by law and that I do not now belong to and that I will not, while I shall hold the said office, belong to any association, society, or confederacy formed for or engaged in any seditious purpose, or any purpose tending to disturb the public peace, or in any way disloyal to our Sovereign Lady the Queen and that I will not, while I shall hold the said office, engage or take part in the furthering of any such purpose, or take or administer, or assist or be

*present at or consent to the administering of, any oath
or engagement or binding myself or any other person
to engage in any such purpose."*

It is obvious that it is the mention of Almighty God and the pledge
of loyalty to the head of the British state, Her Majesty the Queen,
which was deemed as being so unacceptable. That's is why it had
to be replaced by an oath of allegiance to the European Human
Rights Act.

The new oath says….

*"I hereby do solemnly and sincerely and truly declare
and affirm that I will faithfully discharge the duties of
the office of constable, with fairness, integrity, diligence
and impartiality, upholding fundamental human rights
and according equal respect to all individuals and their
traditions and beliefs; and that while I continue to
hold the said office I will to the best of my skill and
knowledge discharge all the duties thereof according
to law."*

It was particularly depressing when this traitorous change to
policing received the Royal Assent in 1998 from Her Majesty
the Queen. Patten's review of policing had been sold by the peace
processors as a way to take politics out of policing. In fact, on
the day on which it was published, 9th September 1999, Patten
himself had the brass neck to state that.

*"We believe that it is possible to find a policing solution
to the policing problem, but only if you take the politics
out of policing. That is a key part of this report - the
de-politicisation of policing."*

Bearing this in mind, he then proceeded to recommend the establishment of a Policing Board stacked with politicians and those selected by politicians, and the simultaneous creation of 26 District Policing Partnership boards, which would also be filled with politicians. It's also interesting to note that, even at this point, Patten was claiming that terrorists could not be recruited into the police. But convicted terrorists were seated on the Policing Board, and a motion to allow ex-terrorists into the District Policing Partnerships was approved without a vote in Westminster in 2003.

In a final insult to the pro-union community, Patten recommended that there should be active employment discrimination in favour of Roman Catholics. This perverse recommendation made sure that Northern Ireland is the only place in western Europe where it is lawful to discriminate against the best qualified candidate seeking a job in the Police Service. The specious argument put forward to justify this obscene legislation was that the low level of Roman Catholics representation in the police force was unacceptable and it did not command the support of the broad nationalist community. This completely ignores the glaring reason why so few Roman Catholics served in the police: namely, years of IRA pernicious intimidation.

There have been many brave Roman Catholics who loyally served in the RUC, with Sir John Gorman being one prominent such figure. Another successful Roman Catholic officer was Chief Superintendent Brian McCargo who spent three decades serving the community in the RUC.

"I was one of the first two officers to enter the RUC reserve as a part-time officer. Not only was I reared in a nationalist area, but I was heavily involved in the GAA (Gaelic Athletic Association). I played Gaelic football for Ardoyne and for my county, Antrim. I was a well

> *known sportsman. As a result of going into the reserve
> I was told to leave the GAA. I was also discouraged
> from living in the area by the paramilitaries. Had I
> persisted in living there, the chances are I'd have been
> shot dead. That's how difficult it was. It's true that if
> you get points for killing a police officer, you get double
> points for killing a Catholic police officer."*

The brutal truth ignored by Patten was that it was republican agitation within local communities that ensured Roman Catholic police officers found it almost impossible to serve. This gave the terrorists the double advantage of being able to portray the RUC as a "Protestant police force" and also to ensure that local intelligence gathering on their nefarious activities was severely restricted. In essence, the unionist community was to be punished because the nationalist community did not support the RUC.

Both the Ulster Unionists and the Democratic Unionists started off from the position that they would not accept the destruction of the RUC for to do so would have been to implicitly accept the poisonous propaganda spewed forth by the IRA. Whether this apparent support for the RUC was out of fixed principle or driven by a fear of electoral consequences can be speculated upon, but it became clear that, despite assurances, David Trimble was prepared to go along with the symbolic and substantive changes proposed by Patten.

Without the Belfast Agreement/Good Friday Agreement, there would have been no Patten report. Without Patten, the RUC's demise would have been much more difficult to bring about. Naturally, there were generous redundancy packages for those RUC officers that wanted to leave, and the RUC itself was awarded the George Cross. The George Cross is the highest gallantry award for civilians as well as for military personnel in actions which are not in the face of the enemy or for which purely military honours would not normally be granted. Only the people of Malta and the Royal Ulster Constabulary have had this award bestowed collectively, but, whilst the RUC fully deserved it, it was of course awarded in memoriam and to spare unionist politician blushes at the disgraceful treatment handed out to the brave men and women who had served in the force.

During the next few years, Northern Ireland haemorrhaged some of its most experienced police officers as they accepted the redundancy packages available and left in disgust. This was to have major consequences for the efficiency of the PSNI, as it found itself lacking the experience that the departing officers had gained over decades. Naturally this was all swept to one side and more media friendly initiatives, such as the PSNI's commitment to ethnic, gay and transgender issues, highlighted to general media approval.

Having stated that they would resolutely oppose the destruction of the RUC, both the UUP and DUP would, in due course, shrug their shoulders, meekly accept it and then embrace the PSNI, and queue up to enter the financially lucrative structures provided to enforce this politically correct IRA-approved police service. Once more, the unionist political class showed their lack of persistence and a serial failure to stand up and force the hand of the UK government. If the UUP and DUP really had cared about the RUC, they could have insisted to government that their continued political participation depended on the retention of the British symbolism surrounding the force.

Unionists should have seen this all coming as it had happened before. The Ulster Defence Regiment (UDR) was formed in 1970. The aim of the UDR was to protect Northern Ireland from terrorist attack by the way of guarding key installations and patrolling the country, carrying out check-points and road blocks as and when required. The UDR was not to take any part in public orders duties or serve outside the province. By the time the UDR went operational on the 1st April 1970 it had a strength of 2440 soldiers of which 946 were Roman Catholics. Soon after internment started in 1971, Roman Catholic soldiers started to be intimidated out of the UDR. Scores of serving UDR Roman Catholics were visited at their homes or day time work places and told to leave. The threats came in many forms; serving members were handed bullets and informed that the next time they would be fired from guns, others had letters, bullets or excrement put through their letterbox or intimidated by telephone. Equally revolting was when they or their family members were refused service in shops or their children insulted and bullied at school.

The risks of being a UDR soldier increased with the murder of members both on and off duty becoming more frequent. The IRA targeting methods became more direct – for example a terrorist came to the door of Sergeant Maynard Crawford's home and on knocking was answered by his nine year old son. At this time the terrorist asked *"Is your Daddy a policeman?"* The boy without realising the consequences replied *"No, he's in the UDR"*. The family at this time didn't realise that in a few short months they were to be left without a father and husband. That is the reality of how the IRA advanced their cause – using an innocent nine year old to obtain information about his dad so they could murder him. What proud Irish patriots they were! Little wonder people in the Republic of Ireland had little time for them.

Throughout this period, the nationalist SDLP agitated against the UDR, and they were finally placated on July 23, 1991 when Conservative Minister Tom King announced to the Commons that, as part of the restructuring of the armed forces, plans had been agreed to merge the UDR with the Royal Irish Rangers. A year later, the merger of the regiments was complete, and the new regiment was to become the Royal Irish Regiment. But that was only the first step.

As a direct consequence of the Belfast Agreement/Good Friday Agreement, on the 1st August 2007, the home battalions of this regiment were disbanded and redundancies handed out in similar style to those handed out to RUC officers. The IRA Army Council remained intact, and those who had served in the IRA now held some of the highest political offices in the land, sitting on the Policing Board and the District Policing Partnerships, overseeing the implementation of law and order.

By far the most immoral aspect of the Northern Ireland peace process was the perversion of justice that saw 449 convicted terrorists released from prison. Amongst this number were several individuals convicted of mass murder. For example, Sean Kelly who carried out one of Northern Ireland's most notorious bombing, strolled free from captivity in June 2000. Kelly had been convicted of bombing a fish shop on the Shankill Road in Belfast in 1993, killing ten people including two children. He served less than a year for each life he took. Michael Stone was released from prison the same year, having been sentenced to a 684-year sentence in 1989 for six murders and five attempted murders. Again, he served less than two years for each human life that he took. Stone, along with loyalist "Director of terror", Johnny Adair, had also been eulogised by Secretary of State Mo Mowlam as *the unsung heroes of the peace process."*

Another one of those set free was terrorist, Norman Coopey, who was jailed for life for the abduction, torture and murder of James Morgan, a Catholic teenager from county Down in 1997. In this gruesome killing, the mutilated remains of sixteen year old James was recovered by RUC divers from a water-filled hole on a farm at Blackstaff Road on the outskirts of Clough, near Castlewellan. He had been savagely beaten, and an attempt was made to burn the body before it was dumped. The sink hole was used by local farmers to dispose of dead farm animals, and an attempt was made to cover up the youth's body in the pit. Coopey walked free from jail three years later.

It is my view that no political advance is so great that it can excuse this monumental and decadent setting aside of justice. The British government, aided and abetted by weak unionist politicians, caved in to this key IRA objective, and so it was that some of the worst terrorists imaginable were able to walk away from justice.

But it did not end there because IRA/Sinn Fein had a further key ambition, and that was to gain effective control over justice and policing. This could be brought about by firstly ensuring that responsibility for this critical function is devolved from Westminster to the Northern Ireland Assembly. Thereafter, it is merely a question of the mathematics of electoral strength to ensure that the likes of convicted IRA bomber, Gerry Kelly, could assume the position of Minister of Policing and Justice for Northern Ireland as a final triumph over law and order. Amazingly, the Democratic Unionists and Ulster Unionists also support the devolution of policing and justice, and their principle objection is when, not if, this should happen. IRA/Sinn Fein plan this to happen by May 2008; the unionist parties seek to delay this. If past form is to be repeated, the date for the devolution of these critical powers will move out a few months past the IRA/Sinn Fein deadline, and there will be some fig-leaf interim arrangement produced to allow unionists to pretend they have seen off the republican agenda, and then IRA/Sinn Fein will grab this lever of power and policing and justice will fall to the very organisation that has systematically undermined the rule of law, murdered and maimed those who sought to uphold it.

This will be presented in the media and by the unionists as further proof that republicans are buying into the institutions of British law. However, when one considers the republican mindset on this, a different picture emerges.

"All our activity is about achieving our primary goal of a free, independent and united Ireland. Legislation for transfer of power has been passed.

- Powers to be transferred have been substantially agreed.

- The model for a Justice department put forward by the British government to the political parties substantially reflects Sinn Féin's model.

- There is a timeframe for transfer of May 2008 in the British government model, with a commitment that the British government "would take the necessary steps to ensure that the timescale for devolution was not delayed".

- There is a new statement on MI5 setting out in detail that MI5 will have no role in civic policing in the North."

Is this the language of a party that seeks to uphold the rule of British law, or the agenda of insurrectionists in Armani suits who seek to subvert the law? Accepting that IRA/Sinn Fein can control policing and justice will be the ultimate insult to those who fought so bravely against this terror cabal. And yet who would say that the DUP will now oppose this development? After all, having once said that IRA/Sinn Fein could only enter government "over my dead body", the very much currently alive Dr. Ian Paisley's promises now mean next to nothing.

True to form, in August 2007, the local media produced a poll showing that the Northern Ireland public believes the new Executive should only be given powers over policing and justice when there is sufficient public confidence. And the gap between the Protestant and Catholic communities on the timetable for the devolution of policing and justice is less than might have been imagined. A total of 43% overall said criminal justice and policing should be devolved to a local Assembly when there is sufficient confidence in local communities. And that scenario was supported by 46% of Protestants and 39% of Catholics questioned on the issue. If this poll is correct, then the unionist community is even keener than Irish republicans to see policing and justice taken away from Westminster and given to an Assembly that may well then have a convicted IRA bomber as the minister or co-minister for these onerous responsibilities.

It is said that the ultimate triumph of the tyrant is achieved when those enslaved not only accept but express thanks for their condition. Tolerating the subversion of policing and justice will put the people of Northern Ireland, unionist and nationalist, into that perilous state.

NO FUTURE?

It's been said that a week is a long time in politics, and, ten years on from the Belfast Agreement/Good Friday Agreement, it's clear that the weak have been representing unionist interests for far too long. The stark reality is that unionism has been changed utterly by the political machinations that culminated in the Belfast Agreement/ Good Friday Agreement and which were then further refined and reinforced by the St. Andrew's Accord. The scale of this change has been incredible to behold and seems irreversible. Even those vehemently opposed to the progress of the peace processors must recognise this fundamental political fact, and it raises a number of key political questions.

How has unionism been moved along so far and so quickly? Has the quality of democracy been strengthened as a result? Is unionism in a stronger, more confident place in 2007 than it was in 1997? What are the likely prospects for unionism as this 21st century further unfolds? How will the unionist political parties evolve? Will Northern Ireland remain part of the United Kingdom, or will it become a place apart? 2016 marks the centenary of the foundation of the Irish Republic; could that mark the final absorption of Northern Ireland into a 32 county republic? What are the prospects for those who value their Britishness? Is it possible that unionism, under the stewardship of the DUP and UUP has been rapidly metastasising into little Ulster nationalism?

The acceleration of unionism to a position where it embraces political partnership with those implacably opposed to the survival of the union has surprised most commentators, delighted others, and disgusted but a few. These truly seismic shifts have occurred across both major unionist parties, first in the Ulster Unionist Party and then in the Democratic Unionists. Positions that were supposedly fixed in political steel dissolved into jelly as u-turns were executed and somersaults performed. Why was this? Might it have been down to the fact that unionists were outmanoeuvred and felt obliged to take the best deal offered to them, no matter how far below their expectation level this lay? Is it at all possible that the political negotiators of the two provincial unionist parties were hopelessly out of their depth when it came to dealing with those first class intellects representing the interests of the British and Irish government?

If we believe the story put across by the representatives of the UUP and DUP, they managed to outflank those battalions of skilled civil servants. Not only did they perform this Herculean feat, but they also ran rings around the SDLP and IRA/Sinn Fein. Just how credible a position is that? Yet, for years David Trimble insisted that he better understood the provisions of the Belfast Agreement/ Good Friday Agreement than all the other parties to it! Ian Paisley ambitiously claimed that the St. Andrew's Accord was the best possible deal for unionists, even though it was substantially the same deal that he had rejected up until the point where his party became lead negotiators!

Whether the democratic process has been strengthened in Northern Ireland rather depends on whether one considers that terrorists have a right to sit in government and influence the direction that the country should take. Now, most reasonable people accept that the IRA are committed terrorists, although their apologists prefer to look upon them as perhaps overly-enthusiastic freedom fighters, motivated murderers if you will. Of course they killed innocent men, women and children and wrecked the economic infra-structure of the country, and of course they engaged in every form of criminality, but they were doing this for a noble cause. Such is the depraved world view of IRA apologists, but, as history is re-written, the IRA is now being presented as the heroic good guys.

Over the decades, most unionists held to the view that the best place for an IRA terrorist was in prison, if not at the end of a noose. The very notion of sharing power with the representatives of an organisation that was slaughtering so many fellow citizens seemed inconceivable not so many years ago. Even the mildest of unionist politicians who may have been attracted to the idea of sharing power with the main constitutional nationalist party, the SDLP, would have recoiled from the idea of putting the IRA terror godfathers into power. But the entire basis of the Northern Ireland peace process has been based on the idea that if the IRA was prepared to scale back its atrocities then it had to be granted not just an admission to the chamber of democracy but also handed the keys to the kingdom.

And so it has been that Northern Ireland's political and public institutions have become overwhelmingly tainted with the whiff of cordite and the scent of semtex as, one by one, they have embraced terrorists' apologists. Insurrectionists are the new establishment, and the question can be posed as to how the quality of democracy is strengthened by rewarding those who wish to use it to pursue their own anti-democratic position?

Fictions have had to be created in order to sustain the illusion that a terrorist inclusive Assembly is an advance for democracy. One of the most deadly of these is the idea that, just because IRA/ Sinn Fein command substantial electoral support amongst the nationalist community in Northern Ireland, this somehow makes them democrats. It doesn't anymore than it did back in the 1930's when the Nazis also enjoyed widespread electoral support. This warning from history has been studiously ignored by the architects of the peace process.

Little attention has been paid to the background of those from IRA/Sinn Fein who have been elected to sit in power in the Assembly. And so it is that convicted killers, convicted bombers, convicted bank-robbers and self proclaimed terrorist commanders merrily co-exist with conventional politicians. This is positioned as the most normal thing imaginable, and, after years of being exhorted by the peace processors to "*leave the past behind*" and "*move forward*", this means consigning the awful reality of those who sit in power over us to the memory hole. It seems to me that democracy has not been strengthened in any way in Northern Ireland; instead it has been perverted, corrupted and twisted into something unrecognisable.

Both of the two unionist political parties now accept the concept and practise of power-sharing with terrorists. What does this do to unionism? After all, in no other part of the United Kingdom would politicians countenance sitting in power with terrorists, so has Ulster unionism changed into something that is now post-unionist? Unionist politicians once placed maintaining the link with the rest of the UK as their primary objective, but not any longer. They now put their tatty pursuit of power first, and the opportunity to build their little empires foremost. Surely it can be seen that the past ten years have revealed them to be little more than Ulster nationalists?

These Ulster nationalists are driven to relentlessly pursue political power at any price, and this is what forces them to make the compromises required to sit in a devolved Assembly. Government could not have been clearer in asserting that the only terms in which devolution could return to Northern Ireland would be if it was in a form that could contain IRA/Sinn Fein and accommodate the key wishes of that organisation. In many ways, the quest for devolution which so consumes unionist politicians is also the trap for the ending the union with Great Britain.

The terms of devolved power were always laced with political poison and yet held such great temptation that both major unionist parties found them irresistible. This overriding pursuit of political patronage and privilege has proven a heady drug for the unionist establishment. The British government was banking on this and time has proven them right. The primary loyalty of too many has been to the crown in their pocket. All that was needed was time, and ten years is a relatively short period in which to have transitioned unionist politicians to the point where they accepted the right of the IRA to sit in government and where they happily engage with the Irish government. Not only do they accept republicans as their colleagues in government, but they actually also collude with Scottish and Welsh nationalists to undermine the sovereign government at Westminster.

What else will these little Ulster nationalists accept in the years ahead? They no longer have issues with IRA terrorists in government. They have long since accepted the destruction of the likes of the Royal Ulster Constabulary and the Royal Irish Regiment. In fact, unionist politicians frequently resort to the bizarre last resort of presenting obvious defeats as stunning victories. It is as if they are contemptuous of their own electorate's ability to see through their lies. So, is Irish unification something they would fight or embrace? The answer is – it depends. If it were suddenly foisted upon them, they would be forced to offer up some token resistance. But that is not a foreseeable possibility, and they all know it. There is absolutely no prospect of Northern Ireland being bounced against its will into a united Ireland, so, when unionist politicians beat their chest and declare this will be over their dead body, there is every prospect of them reaching a very old age.

They create a straw man to knock down in a contrived demonstration of their political machismo. Whilst supporters of the Belfast Agreement/Good Friday Agreement claim that it has secured the place of Northern Ireland in the United Kingdom unless the will of the majority is otherwise, this is merely re-stating the position that has always prevailed but pretending it is in some way a new thing! However, gradualised Irish unification is an altogether different and more tempting proposition for some. Both unionist parties fully understand that this salami-slicing of the union is the preferred policy of the British and Irish governments, the republican movement and all who generally wish to see the removal of Northern Ireland from the union. It assumes that if there is sustained and ever increasing economic social and cultural mixing of north and south, then Northern Ireland will become a de facto part of a united Ireland.

This desired end is not just wishful-thinking, for it is specifically supported by the creation of the North- South Ministerial Council and the all-Ireland implementations bodies that operate under its jurisdiction. Set up under a provision of the Belfast Agreement/ Good Friday Agreement, a supplementary international agreement between the British and Irish governments formally established the six north/south implementation bodies. The supplementary agreement was given domestic effect north and south by the British – Irish Agreement Act 1999, and the North/South Co-operation (Implementation Bodies) (Northern Ireland) Order 1999, respectively.

The Belfast Agreement/Good Friday Agreement 1998, specifies 12 areas of mutually beneficial co-operation. Agreement was reached on six areas in which north/south implementation bodies were to be established, and further areas where north/south co-operation was to be managed through existing agencies. The north/south implementation bodies operate on an all-island basis, and are accountable to the Oireachtas (government of Ireland) and the Northern Ireland Assembly. They are co-sponsored (funded) by the two administrations through the relevant departments, north and south. The bodies are:

1. **Waterways Ireland**

2. **The North/South Language Body**

3. **The Food Safety Promotion Board**

4. **InterTrade Ireland - (The Trade and Business Board)**

5. **The Foyle Carlingford and Irish Lights Commission (FCILC)**

6. **The Special European Union Programmes Body (SEUPB)**

"How harmless", argue the sirens amongst unionist ranks, who queue up to gain well paid positions on these bodies. What possible danger is there in giving the Irish government direct input into waterways, and language? But what comes next?

Well, the answer is that amongst those areas identified for further "co-operation" through existing agencies are: transport, agriculture, education, health, and environment. It's called rolling Irish unification, and too many unionist politicians roll over and go with it.

Does it make unionism stronger if it plays an active part in an emerging all-Ireland administration? One of the criticisms made against those who oppose the direction unionism has taken is that they are "defeatists" who lack the confidence that our political elite seem so full of. However, which general chooses to fight a battle where there is going to be a predetermined outcome? The Belfast Agreement/Good Friday Agreement was the offspring of pan-nationalist intrigue, and the political conditions it created were never aimed at securing the union with Great Britain.

The reality is that unionist political leaders lacked the self confidence to comprehensively reject it, so demonstrating their own innate defeatism and utter failure to show real leadership. Misplaced confidence is as dangerous as a lack of confidence, but the unionist elite fail to appreciate this difference. If they can pass off their failures as success then that gets them past the next election, and, ultimately, such short-term thinking is their primary motivator. They lack the wit to think strategically and to hold long-term objectives.

Unionism does not operate in isolation, of course, and there have been major changes to the constitutional integrity of the United Kingdom since Labour came to power in 1997. The devolution agenda which lies at the heart of the Labour project has implications for Northern Ireland which cannot be wished away. 2007 saw the Scottish Nationalist Party (SNP) replace Labour as the biggest Party within the Scottish Parliament. The SNP are committed to Scotland leaving the United Kingdom, and their position gets stronger with every passing year. The creation of a Scottish parliament allowed the genie to jump out of the bottle as far as maintaining the constitutional stability of the UK is concerned, and it is quite possible that Scotland could get to the point in the next twenty years where it actually does do the hitherto unthinkable and vote to leave the United Kingdom. What then for unionism in Ulster?

We hear much of the Ulster-Scots link, so could it be that Northern Ireland would then seek a new constitutional orbit, linked to Scotland and the Republic of Ireland rather than England? Recent times have shown the DUP embrace the SNP and express admiration for the strides that party has made. There is rather less enthusiasm for the British Conservative party or even the UK Independence Party, both of which seek to maintain the integrity of the United Kingdom. The SNP wants to lead Scotland out of the UK; could unionists end up performing a similar role for Northern Ireland? Alex Salmond, the leader of the SNP has forecast 2017 as a target date for the exodus of Scotland from the UK – given the DUP's admiration for the SNP might they seek to beat him to it – one year earlier?

Unionism has polarised around the two major parties, the UUP and the DUP. The room for smaller parties and independents has vanished as the demise of the UKUP demonstrated. The DUP now finds itself in a dominant position, faced with a seriously weakened UUP. It's impossible to see any significant change in this for some years to come. The DUP has outsmarted the Ulster Unionists to such a degree that most of the talent from the UUP is now found within DUP ranks! With no clear political differentiation, the UUP seems fated to slowly wither away rather like it's ageing support base. The damage done to Ulster unionism as a consequence of the Trimble years was colossal, though some of it was obscured at the time. Sclerotic incompetence over too many years has proven a lethal impediment for any kind of restoration of party fortunes. The DUP benefited from this, learning the lessons that accompany division and internal conflict, and are unlikely to follow the same path.

In a way, one feels some sympathy with those who say David Trimble and his associates took all the pain whilst Ian Paisley has pocketed all the gains, but such is the way of politics, and the electorate have been comprehensive in their endorsement of the DUP right up to the point before it cut a deal with the IRA proxies in Sinn Fein. Ian Paisley's leadership of the DUP will not last forever. His presence has been a stabilising force for the party during tumultuous times, and his larger than life persona has helped keep the lid on most internal pressures. Loyalty to *"the Doc"* verges (literally) on the religious, but this period is slowly coming to an end, and, when it does, the issue then arises as to how the party will readjust to a post-Paisley future.

Peter Robinson will most likely assume the role of leader, after all those years of dutifully playing the role of sorcerer's apprentice. Robinson will have to hold the party together -a party which will still contain a substantial Paisley-ite faction. He seems an adept political operator, so it is probable that the DUP will continue as the dominant political force long after Dr. Paisley has left the scene. So there is little hope for the UUP in this future scenario, and the prospect of a Robinson-led DUP may be an even more appealing prospect to those Ulster Unionists who cannot quite embrace the Paisley-led DUP.

The UUP lacks the talent, the vision and the determination to pose a serious challenge, and will do well to even sustain its already weakened position. For years, people argued that unionism should now speak with one voice, and now it does. The problem lies with what that voice is likely to say. Perhaps a glimpse of the future was on display in Washington in late June 2007, when a smiling Peter Robinson and a grinning Martin McGuinness stood shoulder to shoulder in a very public display of the DUP/IRA/Sinn Fein governing axis. Attending the Smithsonian festival, Mr. Robinson said:

"We have been working together for nearly two months and we haven't had a row. It might be good for headlines and news programmes, but there is genuine work being done for the people of Northern Ireland."

Here was clear proof that the DUP and IRA/Sinn Fein are amicable partners in government, with Robinson emphasising that it's all about "working for the people of Northern Ireland". If that is the case, why did the DUP go through a pantomime of refusing to do this since 1997? Why did it have to wait until *after* the March '07 election for this sudden desire to work together for the people to assert itself?

It appears that the brass-neck DUP strategy has been to take the sudden plunge into power-sharing with those who seek to end the union, claiming that this is the best defence of the union. The DUP are banking on the fact that there will be no Assembly elections for several years and that the pro-Union electorate will get used to the Chuckle Brothers road show and whatever follows it during this prolonged period. Using cheap stunts such as deferring water rates for a further year are populist measures aimed at lulling the voters into forgetting the fact that all the political parties opposed any form of increased water rate. With the UUP unable to mount any effective electoral challenge, and the media delighted to see this political marriage, years of positive media headlines can be counted upon to convey the impression that Ulster is safe in the hands of the DUP.

IRA/Sinn Fein are naturally delighted at roll-over unionism exhibited by the DUP. Several republicans have commented that even they were not quite prepared for the enthusiastic approach that Dr. Paisley and his colleagues have taken to power-sharing. No wonder that Martin McGuinness appears to have had a Joker-like fixed grin of his face! When an organisation that is explicitly committed to the ending of the union praises its new-found unionist partner in power, surely even the most doe-eyed believer of DUP tall tales must wonder what is happening? Has the republican movement quietly given up on its' objective to remove Northern Ireland from the United Kingdom? Not according to any leading republican, but perhaps the DUP leadership know better?

Looking forward, the DUP/IRA/Sinn Fein juggernaut seems set to roll all over the local political scene. With the UUP and SDLP looking like spent political forces, it is hard to see what they can do to de-rail the unholy power-sharing alliance. It would be healthier for the state of democracy if the UUP and SDLP could revive their fortunes and provide a form of meaningful opposition as well as offering the electorate fresh choices. But I don't see this happening, or at least not under current management.

The Mark Durkan-led SDLP seems to flirt with trying to out green IRA/Sinn Fein, whilst the UUP occasionally tries to offer an alternative to the DUP but then blows it by seeking to retain its' presence in the Executive. In September 2007, Irish Prime Minister, Bertie Ahern, announced that his party, Fianna Fail, would organise in Northern Ireland. Some suggest that it may end up merging with the SDLP as a way of bolstering the non-IRA/Sinn Fein vote within the nationalist community. The SDLP leader, Mark Durkan, welcomed this as a positive development and said….

> **We now have the possibility of new alignment within northern politics and on a north-south basis. We don't want to pursue either at the expense of the other, because both are part of the positive change of opening up the new political landscape."**

Unionists might wonder why the main political party in the Republic of Ireland now sees fit to stand for election in Northern Ireland. Fianna Fail is committed to bringing about Irish unity, so why is it now organising in Northern Ireland when the position of the union is allegedly so secure?

The implications of all of this from a unionist point of view are disturbing since it all suggests that the DUP has no sense of shame over its enthusiastic embrace of IRA/Sinn Fein. It appears to have concluded that that it can do what it wants with little real opposition and virtual electoral impunity. Since the DUP is driven by a desire to maximise the political power it can leverage, it will continue to find ways to work with republicans lest the wheels come off the gravy-train. With MLA noses deep in the trough of financial largesse, it seems inconceivable that they will voluntarily remove them. Republicans have less to lose than financially rapacious unionists, and so the dynamic will always revolve around what concessions the DUP will make to keep things going forward. And I forecast there will be many concessions along the road.

There are several areas that should prove interesting to observe. The DUP has dismissed the idea of an Irish Language Act being made law and has made clear that it will veto an Irish Language Act. Gregory Campbell, MLA for East Londonderry and one of the Ian Paisley's closest associates, said there needed to be more money for the development of the Ulster-Scots language. This curious logic then concludes that because there is not enough money for the Ulster-Scots language, there cannot be progress in making the Irish Language Act law. IRA/Sinn Fein see this Irish Language Act as being absolutely central to their project of "greening" Northern Ireland and naturally the UK government fully buys into this. Draft plans issued by the Department of Culture, Arts and Leisure in March envisage the appointment of an Irish language commissioner and the establishment of Irish language schemes for public bodies. It's also worth understanding that the provision for the Irish Language Act was part of the St. Andrew's Agreement embraced by the DUP. Gerry Adams said he personally negotiated the Act during the St. Andrew's talks with the Prime Minister and the Secretary of State, so it is hard to see how he will accept the glib dismissal of this by the DUP.

Such diametrically opposed viewpoints are guaranteed to cause friction between these new found partners in power, and I suggest that the likely compromise will mean the elevation of the Irish language to the position required by IRA/Sinn Fein whilst more money is magically found to be poured into Ulster-Scots coffers. Such a deal will be presented as a win-win; the DUP will try and sell the idea to their electorate that whilst it had to concede the principle of the elevation of the Irish language to equal status with the English language, it has succeeded in getting more money for the Robbie Burns appreciation society. Big deal!

The planned devolution of policing and justice powers from Westminster to the Northern Ireland Assembly will also prove a contentious battleground. IRA/Sinn Fein envisage a situation where, by 2009 latest, this transfer of powers will have taken place, and one of its delegates may hold this symbolic and hugely important ministerial office. The DUP appear coy about it and seek to long-finger the day of reckoning. It is easy to see why, as it presents huge presentational difficulties for the DUP even though, were such powers transferred in 2008, there would be no requirement for another Assembly election until 2011, so people could get used to the idea.

If unionists can now tolerate Martin McGuinness as Deputy First Minister, given his publicly stated record of pride in the actions of the IRA, perhaps they could accept the prospect of another IRA convict, such as Old Bailey bomber Gerry Kelly, as Minister for Policing and Justice? What message would this send to those in the legal profession and in the ranks of the forces of law and order who risked life and limb to fight the very people now placed in charge of them through the collusion of unionist political representatives? The betrayal of these brave people would be complete. I believe this is likely to happen but that every effort will be made to sanitise this and present it as a very reasonable compromise. Transition mechanisms may be used to lock the devolved levers of power into place before they are handed over to IRA/Sinn Fein.

The alleged "peace process" has always been about one very simple thing and that is buying off the IRA at all costs. The British government, aided by the Irish government, and supported by the usual culprits in the EU and UN, has managed to cloak this nauseating appeasement in the guise of peace. Unionist politicians are well aware of this, but yet, when brought into the presence of political power, their principles dissolve and they betray their avowed declaration to defend the union.

In 1998, the Ulster Unionist Party struck a deadly blow to the future of unionism by embracing IRA/Sinn Fein. Just under ten years later, the Democratic Unionist Party also rolled over and accepted the key requirement to share power and work with IRA/Sinn Fein. During those years, both unionist tribes swore that the IRA would never win. Now, both unionist tribes embrace the IRA's proxies in Sinn Fein and call them colleagues, so who has won?

Where now for unionism? With both main political parties committed to working with those who explicitly seek to remove Northern Ireland from the union with Great Britain, it strikes me that carefully managed decline and eventual absorption into a united Ireland is the inevitable path that will be taken. Unionist politicians are rather like the Bourbons – they forget nothing and they learn nothing. With a certain skill in presenting defeat as victory, they can look forward to years of pretending the notion they have secured the union even as every aspect of it is unraveled. They will resort to the "Plan B" excuse employed by the DUP to explain its own trooping into power with IRA/Sinn Fein. The fearsome "Plan B" excuse is that that the UK government will impose an unspecified draconian solution upon poor unionists unless they comply with what the government wants. So, no matter how bad a deal unionists get, they will always claim it would have been much worse had the awesome "Plan B" been implemented!

The point in being a unionist is to make the defense of the union with Great Britain the dominant political priority. There are many everyday unionists who do see the need to put the union first, but sadly too many put their faith in a political class which is Vichy in nature and opportunistic in outlook. They are quite happy to be selling Northern Ireland for the pound. From 1997 to 2007, we have witnessed a decayed unionist elite failing to carry out their duty to the pro-union people. Appeasement of evil terrorists has been accepted as a price worth paying to facilitate the return of political power to the Stormont Assembly. It was wrong to do this in 1997, and it's still wrong in 2007.

No matter how many might wish otherwise, no matter how disingenuous the media is in its' portrayal of what has taken place over the past decade, a peace purchased by betraying the central tenets of democracy is a sordid and worthless prize. As the prophet Jeremiah put it thousands of years ago…

"They have healed also the hurt of my people slightly, saying, Peace, peace; when there is no peace."